WOUNDED TRAVELER: DEVOTIONS FOR THE JOURNEY

By Georgia Miller

Author of "Making A Quilt Out of Cobwebs"

Copyright 2009

ISBN 978-0-557-08060-1

"You keep track of all my sorrows. You have collected all my tears in Your bottle. You have recorded each one in Your book." (Psalm 56:8) (NLT)

SPECIAL THANKS!

It is impossible to travel this road by yourself and those who go with you can never be thanked enough. My companions on this long journey (and through life) are Joyce and Ruth. Many thanks also to my friend, Donna, who added all the commas I forgot in this book and my counselor, Alice, who guided me through many dark days and nights.

INTRODUCTION

A dear friend of mine told me not too long ago that during a very traumatic period in her life she had been unable to read the Bible. The effort and energy it took to seek out some passage that could speak to her just wasn't there. She said she kept saying to God, "You know my heart." It reminded me of my darkest hours when I told God more than once, "You've said You love me and that I am Your child. You will need to show me because I can't feel it" and He did by a soothing peace that only He can give.

God's plan for each one of us includes giving us opportunities to trust Him even when they appear to only wound us more. He continues to lead us even when we don't see Him out in front and when His methods seem obscure. Building faith and getting to know God intimately as He desires requires a journey through the deserts of our lives but He has been on this journey already and knows the way.

CROSSING THE RED SEA

Isn't there a way to go,
A way not long and dusty?
A shorter way, more pleasant way,
Where the end is there in view?

The desert is a lonely place
With companions of fear and confusion
God leads on, to where, who knows?
I just know I can't stop here.

He has a plan hidden from me;
 My task to keep on walking.
The cloud leads by day, the fire by night
Is the journey just beginning?

The road is so much longer this way
My feet, my heart so weary.
I've gone so far along this road but
Fear draws me back to Egypt.

Death behind, the sea ahead
Where am I to go now?

My human eyes see no way out

Was I just brought here to perish?

But then the cloud, it moves behind

The danger there obscured.

The east wind blows, waters open wide

The path is clear before me.

Certain death behind, the unknown ahead

Will I choose to walk on dry land?

In spite of the fear, the dread, the doubt

Will I follow close behind Him?

How can I make my dead legs move

Seeing walls of water beside me?

One step at a time, move forward, move on

There's only one way and that's onward.

This, I see is the meaning of faith

Walking on through walls of water.

Seeing through tears the cloud up ahead

My eyes on the back of my Father.

YOU ARE NOT ALONE

"As I was with Moses, so I will be with you; I will never leave or forsake you." (Joshua 1:5)

During my darkest hours, I felt that God had abandoned me. My thoughts were, "God, if I am Your daughter, why didn't You stop this from happening to me?" In spite of my pain and confusion over His seeming lack of concern, I buried myself in the Psalms. There, David cries out to God, pouring out his pain, confusion, and anger. I felt so alone and abandoned. If I couldn't trust God to stay by my side, who could be trusted? Slowly and gently God began to show me that He had been there right beside me all the time and during the darkness was holding me in His arms. He wasn't at all uncomfortable with the emotions I felt. He gave them to me. He is big enough to hear the pain of His children, when it's directed at Him. I found that what He wanted from me was honesty in expressing them. Then, He could begin a healing process in me. Abandoned? Alone? No, just the opposite. He was never closer than when I started telling Him what I was feeling. He wants to hear the cry of our hearts expressing our deepest hurts. When you feel abandoned, cry out to your Abba Father. He wants to gather you into His arms and "sing over you" with words of comfort.

NOTES:

UNCHARTED TERRITORY

"If I go up to the heavens, You are there. If I make my bed in the depths, You are there. If I rise on the wings of the dawn, if I settle on the far side of the sea, even there Your hand will guide me; Your right hand will hold me fast." (Psalms 139:8-10)

My husband's betrayal threw me into an unknown place, a world of pain and confusion, a world I never wanted to be in. Did God know where I was? Was I alone in that new world or was He there, too? I began to realize that the God I thought I knew wasn't the God of reality. I discovered that I knew a lot *about* God but did not have the intimacy with Him that He so desires. That lack of intimacy kept me from feeling-knowing that He was with me no matter where I was. He wasn't going to let me be "lost". Patiently He is teaching me about the relationship that He wants with me and I am beginning to be content knowing that I will be learning about it for the rest of this life and on into the next. *Wherever* you are, He is there.

NOTES:

TRUTH VS. LIES

"You have been a refuge for the poor, a refuge for the needy in his distress, a shelter from the storm and a shade from the heat. For the breath of the ruthless is like a storm driving against a wall and like the heat of the desert. (Isaiah 25:4-5)

A woman whose husband has betrayed her has suffered abuse because of the damage to her sense of personal value and self-worth. Emotional abuse causes a person to question their value. We've all heard the saying, "Sticks and stones can break my bones but words can never hurt me." Whoever came up with that phrase is deaf or just not listening. Emotional abuse is all about the wounds caused by words and the possibility of irreparable damage done to a person's self-worth. In order to battle this attack on our self-esteem and value, we need to begin to recognize the lies that we have accepted as truth. Our betrayal can cause us to question ourselves in many ways, automatically accepting the negative. The way we combat that is to hold the idea up to God's truth. Only then can we see it for what it is. One of the greatest lies is that somehow it is the fault of the one abused! No matter what, this is never the case! We have to look to God to find out what our true worth is in *His* eyes.

NOTES:

WHAT'S WRONG WITH ME?

"For You created my inmost being; You knit me together in my mother's womb. I praise You because I am fearfully and wonderfully made; Your works are wonderful, I know that full well."
(Psalms139:13-14)

One of the first questions we ask ourselves after finding out about our husbands' sexual struggles or addiction is this: What is wrong with me? Why is it that we automatically assume the fault lies with us? It's the built-in rejection of unfaithfulness, of turning away from ourselves and toward something or someone else that prompts the asking of the question. We think that surely if there was nothing wrong with us he would not have gotten involved in another way. One of the reasons we ask the "what's wrong with me" question has to do with our self-esteem and our value, our worth. We feel like we've been thrown out like a sack of garbage with just that much care and concern. Every part of us is critically examined by us and sometimes by others. The questions we ask ourselves go on and on as we try to make sense of why we have been rejected thinking if only we could understand maybe we could fix it. Perhaps then the pain would go away. There is only one "truth" about our value/worth and that is through God's eyes. No other opinion matters: It's truth vs. lies. Believe the truth; that you are wonderful!

NOTES:

PEELING THE ONION

"You have heard these things; look at them all. Will you not admit them? From now on I will tell you of new things, of hidden things unknown to you." (Isaiah 48:6)

None of us likes to admit that we've been wrong or have done sinful things affecting us and others. Admission of guilt takes a strength and courage seldom found within us. The grace of God is what enables us to make those admissions and then to face the consequences. By His grace He also allows us to admit one by one those things He brings to mind; not the whole avalanche because that would kill most of us. As we recover from our woundedness, those admissions are like peeling the layers off an onion. The easiest ones are first followed by increasingly more deeply buried ones. Each layer is accompanied by tears. As each layer is peeled off, there is more grace given which then enables more admissions. We would all like to think that we're able to handle things on our own but our woundedness can only be healed by God's grace.

"My grace is sufficient for you, for My power is made perfect in weakness." (II Corinthians.12:9)

NOTES:

DON'T LET THE SUN GO DOWN

"In your anger do not sin. Do not let the sun go down while you are still angry; and do not give the devil a foothold." (*Ephesians 4:26*)

I grew up thinking that any expression of anger was only destructive, never healthy, so it has been a difficult thing for me to learn. I have been able to look to Jesus for my example. He was angry and very expressive in the temple courtyards at the money changers. His expression didn't equal sin. He was responding to sinful acts by others. (John 21:12-13) In recovering from my own trauma I have discovered that emotions themselves are neither positive nor negative; it is the reactions caused by those emotions that can be the problem. Anger can be a normal response to an offense against us and, as such, needs to be expressed in healthy ways, mostly just by being honest about our feelings. Not expressing anger doesn't cause it to go away; it's only buried to come out later probably inappropriately. I've found that talking about how I'm feeling, while stressful, is very freeing and doesn't allow things to build up to an unmanageable level. By addressing it before bedtime (before the sun goes down) we take charge of it rather than it taking charge of us.

"Hear my prayer, O God; listen to the words of my mouth. Surely God is my help; the Lord is the One who sustains me." (*Psalms 54:2,4*)

NOTES:

ANXIETY VS. PEACE

"Do not be anxious about anything, but in everything by prayer and petition, with thanksgiving, present your requests to God. And the peace of God which transcends all understanding will guard your hearts and minds in Christ Jesus." (*Philippians4:6-7*)

When uncertainty lurks around every corner, anxiety can become an almost constant companion. When the reasons for the anxiety are ever-present, how can a person not be anxious? Dealing with anxiety is another thing (in a long list) that I have been learning about. My anxiety got to a place where there was a lot more of it than there was of anything else. I became jumpy and easily frightened. Anxiety led to paranoia along with the inability to sleep. I knew the verse about *"being anxious for nothing"* but it wasn't helping. There was a period of about 3 months when I prayed these verses every day. I needed to verbally give my concerns, my anxiety to God. One day I realized that I wasn't anxious and it was because God had answered my prayers. The circumstances weren't any different but I knew that God was in charge and He promised that He would not only hear my prayers but would *"guard my heart and my mind"* against the anxiety. Now, when anxiety creeps in again, I am able (not always sooner rather than later) to think about that verse and to claim the peace that guards my heart and mind because I am in Christ Jesus. I can't handle the anxiety or worry but God can. In fact, He's the *only* One who can!

SHAMING MESSAGES

"Therefore, there is now no condemnation for those who are in Christ Jesus." (Romans 8:1)

When I was a child, I was teased by other children saying, "Georgia Porgie, puddin' pie kissed the boys and made them cry." As an adult, that's just a silly rhyme and without knowing what it meant, I was embarrassed and shamed by it. Feeling ashamed is generated by spoken or unspoken messages from others regarding their opinion of who we are as a person. Shaming messages, many times from childhood, worm their ways into our minds and hearts and we begin to think that we really are bad; that what others say about us is true. When we are betrayed, it seems we automatically take on the shame of our husband's addiction. We believe the shaming lies that it's our fault. When we are bowed low with shame and our opinion of ourselves is at its lowest, God lifts our heads. When He lifts our heads, we look into His face and see His eyes of love. His opinion of us is the only one that really matters and all others are insignificant in comparison. Look into God's eyes and see who you really are!

"But You are a shield around me, O Lord, You bestow glory on me and lift up my head." (Psalms 3:3)

NOTES:

MADE NEW

"You were taught, with regard to your former way of life, to put off your old self, which is being corrupted by its deceitful desires; to be made new in the attitude of your minds, and to put on the new self, created to be like God in true righteousness and holiness." (Ephesians 4:22-24)

Every once in a while I catch myself saying, "Oh, that makes me so mad!" I began to realize that nothing and no one can *make* me mad. I allow myself to be mad just as I allow myself to get sucked into various other negative attitudes. I find that I let circumstances, situations, and people push me in the direction of discouragement, discontent, criticism, ungratefulness, apathy, etc. I don't have to allow myself to stay in those bad attitudes. My problem is that subconsciously I feel like I have the *right* to feel however I feel. So, first of all, I have to give up my right to have a bad attitude and then I have to give up the attitude and the reason for it. I don't really like it but while I am not responsible for the things that cause them, I am responsible for my attitudes about those things. Sometimes I would like to just give in to self-pity or the desire to gossip (or whatever) but I know that in the end those things will come back to bite me and the whole thing will be compounded. It will end up being a bigger deal than in the beginning. God provides us with a guard on our attitudes as we tell Him everything: How we're feeling, what we're thinking, everything. He knows it already. What are we waiting for?

UNMASK

"The law of the Lord is perfect, reviving the soul. The statutes of the Lord are trustworthy, making wise the simple." (Psalms 19:7)

I wonder if any of us realize how many different protective masks we wear every day. When we go to church we may wear the "everything is wonderful; I have no problems" mask. When we go to a party we may wear the "jolly, life of the party" mask. Name the situation and we probably have a mask that looks good and fits perfectly. The problem is that no one really knows us because our masks are firmly in place only allowing people to see us on the outside, not who we really are. I understand that there is a danger in being open and vulnerable; not everyone is trustworthy. But the greater danger lies in no one ever knowing us; in never being able to share our pain or our joy. There is never intimacy as long as the masks are on and intimacy is what is desperately lacking in our lives. We have to be honest with ourselves first, of course, and that can be a painful process but God will walk closely with us. During a crisis in our lives, we need to find those trusted sisters that we can be "real" with. Unless we're honest with ourselves and each other, there can be no healing. That's an important part of recovery.

"The Lord is my light and my salvation---whom shall I fear? The Lord is the stronghold of my life---of whom shall I be afraid?" (Psalms.27:1)

NOTES:

TOO HEAVY

"Therefore, since we are surrounded by such a great cloud of witnesses, let us throw off everything that hinders and the sin that so easily entangles, and let us run with perseverance the race marked out for us." (Hebrews 12:1)

A few years ago I saw an illustration of the emotional baggage we can carry around with us. A woman entered the room carrying numerous bags of all sizes, nearly staggering under the weight. Each bag was identified as anger, bitterness, depression, and others. The baggage was preventing her from walking upright. Even her face reflected the great weight she was carrying. She staggered to a cross at the far side of the room and, taking the bags one at a time, confessed that she was carrying it, laying it at the foot of the cross. Soon, she was standing straight and tall, not nearly buried in bags. She was free from the burden of her baggage, a burden Jesus never intended for us to carry alone. The challenge is to recognize what baggage we are carrying and then to be willing to give it up. We have carried some of our bags for so long that they have nearly grown into our skin, becoming part of who we are. Those will be harder to lie down but just imagine the relief of not carrying all that weight any more!

"Jesus said, 'Come to me, all you who are weary and burdened, and I will give you rest. Take my yoke upon you and learn from me, for I am gentle and humble in heart, and you will find rest for your souls.'"
(Matthew11:24)

FIGHT FOR IT

"For our struggle is not against flesh and blood, but against the rulers, against the authorities, against the power of this dark world and against the spiritual forces of evil in the heavenly realms."
(Ephesians6:12)

We've all heard the saying "Anything worth having is worth waiting for." Well, in the world of recovery it's "Anything worth having is worth *fighting* for." The battle against addictions, against losing a marriage, against all of the losses associated with moral failure has to be fought in order to be won. This is a battle for souls and that's why we can believe that while it looks like we're fighting against people, what we're really fighting against is the enemy and his desire to destroy us. What better way to cause destruction in a person's life, in a marriage, in the church, in all relationships than to open all the doors to temptation and things of the flesh? There is no victory without a battle and our victory has already been won. God has fought the battle with sin and death and the victory is His through Christ Jesus and His sacrifice on the cross. We fight the battle daily after putting on the armor that God provides (Ephesians 6). There is no battle so great that God can't win. It may look like the enemy is winning from time to time but the battle is already won!

NOTES:

PROVE IT

"Those who know Your name will trust in you, for You, Lord, have never forsaken those who seek You." (Psalms 9:10)

In order to "believe" in someone there has to be some evidence that assures us our belief is not misplaced. My trust in my husband was put to death when he confessed his sexual addiction to me. I didn't know if I could ever believe anything he said again. For a long time I just assumed I couldn't, that everything he said was a lie. Trust can be rebuilt but only as we're able to observe changes being made over time. We can eventually come to a place where there can be a measure of belief that recovery is progressing. The larger issue though is who we're actually placing our trust in? If our hope, faith, belief, or security is in a person we will always be disappointed. People fail each other. We don't fail each other in the same ways, but we will hurt each other simply because of our humanity. We are not infallible but Jesus is. He is the One we can believe, the One who never lies and never fails us. He is worthy of our belief. This was really the greater battle for me, believing that God had not walked away but was there all the time. I could check Him out and see if He had proven Himself over time. Then I could believe.

"Trust in the Lord with all your heart and lean not on your own understanding; in all your ways acknowledge Him, and He will make your paths straight." (Proverbs 3:5-6)

ROOT OF BITTERNESS

"See to it that no one misses the grace of God and that no bitter root grows up to cause trouble and defile many." (Hebrews 12:5)

It's very hard to work through all the emotions resulting from being deeply wounded. There are so many of them and they seem to be out of control. Some fade over time without any residue but anger is not one of them. Unresolved anger results in bitterness which is only a short step from vengeance. Bitterness takes root in our hearts as we don't face our hurts and anger. Hurt and anger are like a cancer growing inside our hearts, soon infecting our whole body and spirit. It starts inside but eventually shows up outside in our faces and our behaviors. Life takes on a dark tone and nothing is ever very good. Many times cancer can be healed because it is discovered early. So it is with anger. We can avoid bitterness by working through the anger before it can grow into something cancerous. Pushing our emotions away and not grieving our losses fully can also cause us to be bitter. It affects our lives and all of our relationships. It's only by accepting God's grace that we can avoid bitterness ruining our lives. Very gently He shows us that the one who has hurt us so badly needs forgiveness and mercy and in that sense is no different than we are. The grace that God offers is the one thing that can save us from being swept into bitterness.

NOTES:

THE BLAME GAME

"Do not accuse a man for no reason---when he has done you no harm." (Proverbs 3:30)

Many times people are responsible for our pain but there can come a point at which we rely on blaming other people or situations for our own bad behaviors and the choices we make on our own. When we can blame someone else we relieve ourselves of that responsibility. When a person takes responsibility for their own actions it means they have looked those actions in the face, acknowledged them, and accepted God's grace and forgiveness. Blame is like quicksand dragging us slowly under; sucking the life out of us. God throws us a rope, a rope of responsibility, and all we have to do is take it.

"Guard my life and rescue me; let me not be put to shame, for I take refuge in You."(Psalms 25:20)

NOTES:

NO BLIND -SPOTS

"Jesus said, 'How can you say to your brother, 'Brother, let me take the speck out of your eye, 'when you yourself fail to see the plank in your own eye.' You hypocrite, first take the plank out of your eye, and then you will see clearly to remove the speck from your brother's eye.'"
(Luke 6:42)

In recovery there can be no blind -spots. Everything must be examined honestly and completely. Anything less will be considered allowance or even acceptance of behaviors. The pain we feel can cloud our vision so that we don't or aren't able to see ourselves and our attitudes clearly. For a long time I thought "Well, I haven't done anything like what **he** did" implying that I was somehow "better", not a sinner in my own heart. I finally realized that my righteousness was based on my opinion, not God's. God judges each one of us according to our own deeds. He sees us as the individuals He created us to be. He doesn't compare us to one another like we do. God is gentle and He will patiently show us what parts need to be pruned so our recovery can be healthy and complete.

"I pray that out of His glorious riches He may strengthen you with power through His Spirit in your inner being." (Ephesians 3:16)

NOTES:

FENCES

"The boundary lines have fallen for me in pleasant places; surely I have a delightful inheritance." (Psalms 16:6)

Most of us have a struggle saying "no" to others. We're asked to be on a committee or be in charge of an activity at church and we automatically say "yes". Someone calls us just as we're leaving the house to talk and we can't say "I'll have to call you back." Everyone roams around freely in our lives because we have no fences to keep them out. Those fences are called "boundaries" and need to be in place for our protection and to enable us to use the gifts God gave us instead of flying off in all directions, doing all manner of other things, because we can't say "sorry, no." Boundaries allow us freedom to work in our areas of giftedness and enable us to do a good job at what we do rather than a half-hearted job at a lot of things we shouldn't be doing. As we begin to find out what it means to set boundaries in our lives, we will find a peace that we weren't experiencing before. Think of it as peace vs. chaos.

"I will lie down and sleep in peace, for You alone, O Lord, make me dwell in safety." (Psalms 4:8)

NOTES:

TINY PIECES

"The Lord is close to the brokenhearted and saves those who are crushed in spirit." (Psalms 34:18)

"My heart and dreams are shattered; my world in tiny pieces. I feel so abandoned, so alone." This is the opening line to a poem I wrote when my heart was broken. It felt like it was a mirror broken into a million pieces that could never be put back together again. "Humpty Dumpty sat on a wall. Humpy Dumpty had a great fall. All the King's horses and all the King's men couldn't put Humpty together again." This is the time when all you can do is hold on to God for dear life and cry. I wanted my world to be "back to normal" again so desperately but it just didn't happen. God is the only One who can heal a broken heart and in His time He will do it; it just won't be easy or quick. It heals from the inside out so every part has to be knit back together again very slowly and thoroughly. Some days it will feel as though nothing has changed and you'll never smile again. It's only in looking back that you see any progress at all, but one day you'll notice that you have actually laughed at some silly thing the dog did. Even though it feels awkward, you will know that your heart can be mended again.

NOTES:

BRUISED

"But He was pierced for our transgressions, He was crushed for our iniquities; the punishment that brought us peace was upon Him, and by His wounds we are healed." (Isaiah 53:5)

God understands being bruised and broken. Because He has experienced pain Himself, He can identify with our brokenness. His pain has brought us healing! The bruising of our hearts and spirits isn't easy to see, but that doesn't make it any less real than actual black and blue marks. The aching, hurting feeling will take time to ease. We seek healing in a lot of ways, sometimes even denial, but the only real healing comes from God and over time He can turn even that into something that can be used for good. When we feel alone in our wounded condition, we can take comfort knowing that God has been there already.

"A bruised reed He will not break; and a smoldering wick He will not snuff out. In faithfulness He will bring forth justice." (Isaiah.42:3)

NOTES:

TOO BUSY?

"Sow your seed in the morning and at evening, let not your hands be idle, for you do not know which will succeed, whether this or that, or whether both will do equally well." (Ecclesiastes 11:6)

Keeping busy has its pros and cons. It can help you focus on something besides your pain for a period of time or it can be used to avoid going through the pain and the healing process. We have a natural aversion to pain and try to avoid it at all cost. When we have a headache we run to the aspirin bottle. When our muscles ache we get out the Ben-Gay. It's the same with emotional pain; we try to escape it by various means. Keeping really busy is one of those and should be used sparingly as a pain remedy. Busyness can also prevent us from seeing God's hand and direction in our recovery. We can miss the very things that would show us His love and care.

"I will praise the Lord, who counsels me; even at night my heart instructs me." (Psalms 16:7)

NOTES:

CALMING THE STORM

"Jesus said, 'Do not let your hearts be troubled. Trust in God; trust also in Me. Peace I leave with you; My peace I give you. I do not give to you as the world gives. Do not let your hearts be troubled and do not be afraid.'" (John 14:1, 27)

Believe it or not, we have a choice about how we feel or how we respond to how we feel. Our emotions can feel very much out of control, but that is only because we have let go of the reins and the horses are running wild. The verse says, "**Do not**..." which is a very clear indication that we **do** have a say; we **can** have calm spirits and peaceful hearts. We have to work for them, but they are available when we call on God for **His** peace. We have a saying in our family: "When in danger, when in doubt; run in circles, scream and shout." This is just the opposite of the calm and peace that God can give during times of crisis. During my times of greatest turmoil, if I give that agitation to God, within a very short time it is gone. I don't pretend to know how it happens, but suddenly I feel less anxious and am able to think more clearly; most definitely a "God thing".

"Cast all your anxiety on Him because He cares for you." (I Peter 5:7)

NOTES:

OUR CHALLENGE

"Choose my instruction instead of silver; knowledge rather than choice gold." (Proverbs 8:10)

While recovering from a broken heart is definitely one of the greatest challenges that any of us will face, we can know that God has provided for that to happen. We're not left alone to wonder what in the world to do. The need for focus and looking ahead is ongoing and the work to be done is often hard and painful. There is no quick fix and the time it takes can be discouraging. There will be days, though when the progress can be seen and we are given new energy to go on. Since this kind of recovery is emotional in nature, there are many emotions to deal with and this is a great part of the challenge; to let God help us sort through them. There is a goal that we can strive for and it's one of a healthy life; one that is forward looking and doesn't live in the past. The challenge for all of us is to push against those things that attempt to hold us back.

"I press on toward the goal to win the prize for which God has called me heavenward in Christ Jesus." (Philippians 3:14)

NOTES:

OH NO! CHANGE!

"He who is the Glory of Israel does not lie or change His mind; for He is not a man, that He should change His mind." (I Samuel 15:29)

"Change" implies going a new direction, often unexpectedly. Life has been going on "normally" and suddenly everything is different. Unsettling! Change is a part of life that we would just as soon do without most of the time. Some changes are caused by positive happenings in our lives while others come about through crisis or pain of some kind. Change has a way of taking our lives and throwing them up in the air so that we feel out of control and wondering where we'll land. It produces an uncomfortable, insecure feeling because the tracks of our everyday lives are routine and predictable. At times we may feel we're "in a rut" and that we would like some excitement but only temporarily, not permanently, as in "change". Change may cause things to be out of our control but they are never out of God's. When we wonder what is going on around us and if God is paying any attention to us, we can remember that there is never anything that touches our lives until it has passed through His hand. We see only a small part of life while He sees the entire picture from beginning to end. We can trust Him to see us through any change that comes into our lives and, accepting His hand in our lives, can know that on the other side of that change we will be more like Him.

"Now we see but a poor reflection, then we shall see face to face. Now I know in part; then I shall know fully, even as I am fully known."(I Corinthians 13:12)

EXERCISE TIME

"A wife of noble character who can find? She is worth far more than rubies." (Proverbs 31:10)

A person's character is built into their nature, but like the muscles in our bodies, must be exercised in order to be strong. In recent years we've heard from political circles that "character matters". It seems they're saying that what drives many decisions we make for ourselves and on behalf of others is character. A character of integrity will choose unselfish paths while one with more self-centered motivation will go another direction. For our model in building our character, we have to look to God and study His character qualities. There is no one else who can teach us more about godly character than He. Good character doesn't come to us naturally because we're all born with a bent toward a selfish life style. Building that character is an ongoing, lifelong process built into us by our Teacher and example. Throughout every day and maybe especially during a recovery process, we have many opportunities to use our "character" muscles, to either strengthen or weaken ourselves. God allows these situations to come our way to teach us Christ-like maturity.

"Perseverance must finish its work so that you may be mature and complete, not lacking anything." (James 1:4)

NOTES:

FREEDOM OF CHOICE

"You did not choose me, but I chose you and appointed you to go and bear fruit: fruit that will last. Then the Father will give you whatever you ask in My name." (John 15:16)

We are faced with choices every single day. Most of them are of a simple kind: what shall I wear today? What shall I eat for breakfast? In this country we have freedom to make choices and we not only take that for granted we often abuse the privilege. In the area of behaviors we also have choices to make. These kinds of choices are generally of a more important nature than what to wear that day. They involve our emotional well-being along with affecting those closest to us. I've heard people say they "just couldn't help it." Well, we **can** help it because we have a choice; we just don't **choose** to exercise it. We would rather not accept the responsibility of our bad choices. It is a freedom that we need to choose to appreciate. God gives us freedom of choice and the ability to exercise our free will, but He also gives us guidelines to follow so that those choices will be the ones that are best for us. If we know God's word, we will know those guidelines. They're not hard to miss!

"Choose for yourselves this day whom you will serve. " (Joshua 24:15)

NOTES:

HEALTHY COMFORT

"Praise be to the God and Father of our Lord Jesus Christ, the Father of all compassion and the God of all comfort, who comforts us in all our troubles, so that we can comfort those in any trouble with the comfort we ourselves have received from God." (II Corinthians 1:3-6)

When we are in trouble of some kind, there are various ways we seek comfort: some healthy and some not. Turning to God for His comfort is, of course, the best and most fool-proof but it seems He is not the first One we generally turn to. We usually talk to a family member or close friend; pour ourselves into work; or, run to the refrigerator. How to determine where to turn for comfort is one of the results of asking God for wisdom. During those times of crisis, wisdom from God can help us seek the best kind of comfort; the kind that really helps and doesn't often make things worse. The way that God comforts us is on the inside where any other release we seek is only temporary, outside. The trick is to let go of the reason we need comfort into His capable hands. The comfort that God gives is a healing, soothing salve on our weary, bruised souls. It is a comfort that we can't receive any other way. It is a comfort that in turn we want to pass on to someone else at their time of need.

NOTES:

ALWAYS!

"God is not a man that He should lie, nor a son of man, that He should change His mind. Does He speak and then not act? Does He promise and not fulfill?"(Numbers.23:19)

Years ago when two people agreed on something they would shake hands and that sealed the deal. That was when a man's word meant something and could be trusted. Businesses were built on such agreements and partnerships lasted for generations. Marriages didn't come apart just because people got upset, fell "out of love", or just didn't want to be married any more. There was a commitment to the agreement and it was serious, never taken lightly, as seems is so often the case today. Several years ago, there was a television commercial that had a trademark line, "You've come a long way, baby." Sadly, in so many ways we haven't. Our word is not our bond any longer; even words on documents witnessed by a notary public can't be trusted. There is One whose word can *always* be trusted, who *never* fails, and who *always* keeps His promises-- God. The Bible is full of God's promises, many of which have already come true and there are many more to come. God will *always* keep His word because He cannot lie; it's part of His character: it's impossible. Now, *that* we can count on!

NOTES:

CAN YOU HEAR ME NOW?

"Do not let any unwholesome talk come out of your mouths, but only what is helpful for building others up according to their needs, that it may benefit those who listen." (Ephesians 4:29)

The gift of communication is one that we take for granted. We don't even consider how important it is to us until we lose it. Imagine what it would be like to not hear, see, or be able to speak to those we love. Every time we wanted to talk to someone it would be a struggle or worse yet, impossible. If all of us really used this gift to its fullest, we would not be afraid to let people see the "real" us; we wouldn't fear vulnerability because the wonder of the ability to communicate would be felt in each word and we would make the most of it all the time. There are few places where communication is more important than in a marriage and yet how many times do we see an obviously married couple eating in a restaurant together and not saying a word? Reading the newspaper? Talking on a cell phone to someone else? Relationship is far more than words written on a marriage license. It's the words spoken and then written on our hearts by each other.

NOTES:

APPROACH WITH CONFIDENCE

"Let us then approach the throne of grace with confidence, so that we may receive mercy and find grace to help us in our time of need." (Hebrews 4:16)

When there has been betrayal in a relationship, one of the first things that suffers is a person's sense of confidence in who they are: a person with value and importance. A woman will wonder what is wrong with her that her husband would turn to pornography, affairs, or other methods of acting out sexually. Why couldn't she satisfy him? Wasn't she pretty enough? Slim enough? Questions run through a woman's mind upon discovery of her husband's infidelity. An addict will even use these very questions to try and place the blame on his wife for his betrayal. When we think of that logically, it makes absolutely no sense, but from an emotional standpoint the blow to her confidence makes her wonder if maybe it really is her fault. God understands the importance of confidence and wants us to have that in our relationship with Him. There is no time when we need fear His rejection or disapproval. As we claim that confidence with our Heavenly Father, the confidence about who we are is reinforced. We can become confident that it's God's opinion that really matters!

NOTES:

AVOIDING CONFLICT

"Why do you make me look at injustice? Why do you tolerate wrong? Destruction and violence are before me, there is strife, and conflict abounds." (Habakkuk 1:3)

I have always avoided conflict because I have seen the destructive nature of unrestrained anger and words spoken in the heat of the moment. Conflict resolution is vital in relationships and yet one of the things that is the most difficult for us. Maybe we should be required to take a course to learn how to do it "right" because most of us only know how to do it "wrong" causing more damage than the original point. Conflict is part of the fabric of relationships and yet most of us would avoid it if we could. Conflict, when handled well, can strengthen a relationship; handled poorly can be divisive. It can increase intimacy because of the necessity of real conversation at a level deeper than surface. Believe it or not, conflict can actually strengthen a marriage because of the vulnerability that is necessary to actually share the feelings in resolution. Avoidance of conflict will not make it go away but will cause the issues to go deeper. To learn how to have conflict in the right way is important to a relationship and is part of making a marriage really work well. Honesty is critical in a marriage and hiding your feelings is not being honest. I know; I've done it. It doesn't work!

NOTES:

WHO'S IN CONTROL?

"Like a city whose walls are broken down is a man who lacks self-control." (Proverbs 25:28)

We all like to feel that we are in control of our lives, things around us, and situations that directly affect us. To feel in control gives us a sense of security and the impression that all is right with the world. Things are in order; chaos doesn't reign. Self-control implies boundaries that help us deal in healthy ways with things in our lives or other people's demands on us. There is another kind of control that is not positive but destructive. It is a control that people attempt to exert on others: the way they act, the way they dress, the things they say, even what they think. It is as if the one being controlled has no will or right to act on their own. The one doing the controlling is demanding and domineering although he/she could be a quiet controller, called "passive aggressive". Controllers often act out of the fear that if they don't control those around them there will be a mass exodus; that the only way there can be a safe relationship is if one is holding power over another. They have a need to be in charge: to be stronger, better, more "right" than others and they will go to great lengths to prove their supremacy. In reality none of us is really "in control". God is the only One powerful enough to be in charge and direct the lives of mankind. We just *think* we are.

NOTES:

THE BEST COUNSELOR

"But when He, the Spirit of truth (the Counselor) comes, He will guide you into all truth." (John 16:13)

Counselors are very important in helping us sort through the confusing maze of emotions during the crises in our lives. It's vital that we remember though, that humanly speaking, "one size does not fit all." In other words, not every counselor is right for every client. Just as we may try on several different pairs of shoes before buying, we have to remember that we are not committed to a particular counselor after the first visit. We have the right to make a choice without pressure. Getting referrals and recommendations from friends or other family members can make the task less daunting, but we still have to find out for ourselves if they are a good fit for us. Especially, in the area of sexual addiction not just anyone will do. It has to be someone who is experienced working with people with these kinds of struggles. As opposed to human counselors, though, there is a Counselor that will ***always*** be the right fit, will ***always*** guide us "into all truth" and who ***always*** has an opening in His schedule.

NOTES:

REAL COURAGE

"Be strong and courageous. Do not be terrified. Do not be discouraged, for the Lord your God will be with you wherever you go." (Joshua 1:9)

Courage isn't the absence of fear. To not feel fear in certain situations is foolishness. Courage is action in the face of fear; moving forward in spite of fear that could paralyze. Fear of the unknown, fear of failure, many kinds of fear could stop us dead in our tracks. If we gave in to that fear, we would remain in our homes with all the doors and windows shut and locked. We would never drive on the highways because it is so dangerous. We would never go shopping at night because scary people are out there. Most of the time, we don't stop and think about all the things that we could be afraid of because we know that "life goes on" and we can't avoid life just because we allow ourselves to be afraid. It takes a certain amount of courage just to leave the house every day, but we don't really consider ourselves courageous. We reserve that title for the fireman who runs into a burning building. God knows there are situations that come into our lives that require courage and He reminds us that no matter what, He will be with us, wherever and whatever, no exceptions. He will give us just what we need to move through each day courageously.

NOTES:

FACING THE CRISIS

"The Lord is a refuge for the oppressed; a stronghold in times of trouble." (Psalms 9:9)

At some point in time, everyone has some kind of a crisis come into their life. A crisis comes upon us unexpectedly, out of the blue. We are thrust into it unwillingly and with a sense of powerlessness. Something has happened that has turned our world upside down and suddenly life isn't settled or secure. Some crises come, mess things up for a while, and then life settles down again: We recover. Others are not so easily dealt with. They are the ones where a loved one has been severely injured or has died. Perhaps there has been a divorce or an emotional betrayal such as adultery. These crises require intentional recovery after a period of grieving. Life does indeed go on but not like it was. Major adjustments have to be made and difficult decisions have to be pondered. It is so easy to sink into depression or denial during these times, but God wants us to know that He is always there for us. He is our refuge, our hiding place, our stronghold in times of trouble. There is nothing that He won't go through with us, giving us the strength and courage to confront anything that comes along.

NOTES:

TEARS FROM HEAVEN

"I am worn out from groaning; all night long I flood my bed with weeping and drench my couch with tears." (Psalms 6:6)

For most of my life, I wasn't able to honestly express emotion well and found that I cried at things like Hallmark commercials. I couldn't grieve for real hurts so my grief came out in very superficial ways. At a crisis point in my life, God taught me how to grieve and really, honestly cry for hurts suffered. There were times when I thought I would never be able to stop crying because of so much buried emotion. The tears did stop but would always come again. I obviously had quite a stockpile of tears that needed to be cried. I know now that for every hurt, there are tears that need to flow and those tears are God's way of releasing that hurt. I read a sign on a church reader-board one day that said, "A tear on earth summons the King of heaven." I think about that when I'm tempted to hold my tears in. I let them fall knowing God is on His way to comfort me as only He can.

NOTES:

FACE IT

"But if you harbor bitter envy and selfish ambition in your hearts, do not boast about it or deny the truth." (James 3:14)

Denial is the only way most of us can continue a behavior that is clearly destructive. We develop the ability to completely ignore it or convince ourselves that it isn't really so bad or that we're not hurting anyone. Denial is also used by victims to protect themselves against the reality of the truth and the inevitable pain and consequences of acceptance. The continuing process of denial only increases the emotional damage of the offending behavior resulting in forms of acting out by the victim as well as by the addict. Denial looks truth in the eye and says, "You don't exist." God desires our honesty and integrity in being completely open, beginning with ourselves. Denial of pain cuts us off from God's healing touch and His ability to make us whole.

"He brought me out into a spacious place; He rescued me because He delighted in me." (Psalms 18:19)

NOTES:

DEPRESSION

"All his days his work is pain and grief, even at night his mind does not rest. This too is meaningless." (Ecclesiastes 2:23)

Emotional trauma in our lives can cause several responses, one of which is depression. As the shock of disclosure wears off, the depression sets in because we are faced with the loss of hopes, dreams, even relationships. The type of depression accompanying grieving is fairly normal and can be worked through because it is tied to the circumstances. Healthy grieving is a good antidote to depression. As those circumstances change over time and life becomes livable again, the depression lessens. There were many times when Jesus left His disciples and went off by Himself to be alone with His Father for a time. He was rejuvenated and renewed by their intimacy. I'm not saying He was depressed but that the burdens He carried required restoration of His spirit and He couldn't do it on His own. He chose to let His Father carry those burdens with Him. The burdens that we carry causing depression require attention and sometimes medication. Our spirits need the refreshing restoration offered by God Himself. Go away with Him. Find the rest He offers.

"Be at rest once more, O my soul, for the Lord has been good to you." (Psalms116:7)

NOTES:

NO DISAPPOINTMENT

"And hope does not disappoint us, because God has poured out His love into our hearts by the Holy Spirit, whom He has given us." (Romans5:5)

There will always be opportunities for us to be disappointed with other people. We rarely live up to each others' expectations. Many of our hopes for the outcomes of situations or people's actions are based on wishful thinking rather than on any kind of facts. Sometimes those hopes are based on pure fantasy and would be impossible to fulfill. These are the normal kinds of disappointments--the human kind we face every day. The deeper, more painful kinds of disappointments come at the hands of those we trust the most and are the least expected. The normal kinds come from expectations born within our own minds and hearts. The deeper kinds come because of promises made from another person, i.e. a spouse; promises of love and fidelity that were never meant to be discarded. These are the ones that cut to the soul and affect our ability to love and trust again. The hope that we have in God through Jesus is what we can base our lives on. It will never disappoint or fail us.

"You will be secure, because there is hope; you will look about you and take your rest in safety." (Job.11:18)

NOTES:

DOUBT

"But when he asks, he must believe and not doubt, because he who doubts is like a wave of the sea, blown and tossed by the wind." (James 1:6)

Hand in hand with distrust comes doubt. After a betrayal, there is suddenly nothing about your betrayer that seems to be real and you automatically doubt everything he/she has ever said or the experiences and relationship you have shared. With the admission of a secret life the seeds of doubt are planted and, like weeds, require very little watering to grow very deep roots. To believe again is like a garden; it requires much weeding, watering, and fertilizing for tasty vegetables or beautiful flowers to make their appearance. This is a two person job; one partner cannot do away with doubt without reciprocating changes in behavior. We need never doubt God and His plan for us. His promises are "Yes, and Amen" and will be carried out. All our faith, all our hope, all our trust can be placed in Him because He is faithful and cannot lie.

"Be strong and take heart, all you who hope in the Lord." (Psalms 31:24)

NOTES:

GIFT OF EMOTION

"Have mercy on me, O God, according to your unfailing love;
according to Your great compassion blot out my transgressions."
(Psalms 51:1(

One of the most disconcerting things we experience as we pursue recovery, is the challenge of controlling our emotions. In a lot of instances they rise to the surface and make themselves known in unexpected, unwanted times. Tears appear for no apparent reason; sadness covers us like a cloak. Emotions are amoral which means they are neither bad nor good, they just are. It's what we do with them, the choices we make because of them that matters. Years ago I heard someone say, "You can't stop a bird from flying over your head but you can stop it from building a nest in your hair." We may feel that we have been forced into the emotional condition we're in and to an extent that's true. We still have the option of the more negative reactions taking up permanent residence in our hearts. If we didn't have emotions we would be little more than robots. Think of all the things we would miss if we didn't feel anything. God created us to look in wonder at a sunset, to stand in awe of the might of the ocean, and to cry with delight at the birth of a baby.

"Finally, sisters, whatever is true, whatever is noble, whatever is right,
whatever is pure, whatever is lovely, whatever is admirable---if
anything is excellent or praiseworthy---think about such things."
(Philippians 4:8)

SMELL THE ROSES

"If only my anguish could be weighed and all my misery be placed on the scales! It would surely outweigh the sand of the seas…" (Job.6:2-3)

When a trauma or crisis comes into our lives we can tend to lose much of the ability to enjoy the people we are in relationship with; pets, the beauty of nature, or favorite possessions. Losing our enjoyment of life is like losing the ability to savor flavors via the taste buds on our tongues. I can only imagine how Job felt as he heard of the disasters befalling him and his family; all his losses, one right after another. For a time he sat in sackcloth and ashes, grieving and mourning his family. **Job 42:10, 12** says, *"and the Lord made him prosperous again and gave him twice as much as he had before. The Lord blesses the latter part of Job's life more than the first."* Without a doubt Job never forgot what he had gone through or the loss of his family, but God gave him *"beauty for ashes"* **(Isa.61:3)** and at the end of his life we're told that Job died *"old and full of years"* **(42:17).** Job never forgot but God's grace allowed him to have a full life in spite of his pain. Job learned to enjoy life once again and we can, too. One day you will realize that you're basking in the warmth of the sun and marveling at the colors of flowers once again.

NOTES:

THE GREAT ESCAPE

"When I said, 'My foot is slipping,' Your love, O Lord, supported me. When anxiety was great within me, Your consolation brought joy to my soul." (Psalms 94:18-19)

I was talking to a friend not long ago and her conversation was filled with "I should...." If we listen to ourselves we will hear ourselves saying, "I should be able to....(fill in the blank). These are things that we really can't do but feel that somehow we're failing when we don't. There are times during recovery when we need to just get away, even for just a short time. Escape can be used negatively as a way to avoid pain (denial) but there are times when our minds and emotions need to be put on hold for a while; a good book, a funny movie, or a walk in the park. These activities give our anxious thoughts a rest and a bit of recuperation. Jesus needed to escape from the crowds and noise. He went to the only place He knew He would be refreshed....into the Father's presence. If Jesus needed escape, how much more do we?

"At daybreak Jesus went out to a solitary place. "Luke 4:42

"Jesus went out to a mountainside to pray...." Luke 5:12

NOTES:

FEAR NOT

"So do not fear for I am with you; do not be dismayed, for I am your God. I will strengthen you and help you; I will uphold you with my righteous right hand." (Isaiah 41:10)

Some kinds of crisis can turn our worlds upside down and throw us into an unknown, frightening place, full of scary things. Everything that was once "known" becomes suspect and may appear full of danger. It's the "known" versus the "unknown". Fear can also cause chaotic thinking which slows down our ability to make good choices. Our focus narrows to the point of eliminating anything other than the thing that is causing our fear. God knows how prone we are to fear those things that we are unfamiliar with or cannot control. That's why He tells us over and over again, *"Do not fear for I am with you."* In Isaiah and Jeremiah alone, the words "Do not fear" are repeated 11 times. When God wants us to take special note of something, He repeats it. He wants us to know for sure that He is watching over us. There is nothing we can face that God isn't aware of and in control of. Fear not!

"When you pass through the waters, I will be with you; and when you pass through the rivers, they will not sweep over you. When you walk through the fire, you will not be burned; the flames will not set you ablaze." (Isaiah 43:2)

NOTES:

NO QUICK FIX

"Though You have made me see troubles, many and bitter, You will restore my life again; from the depths of the earth You will again bring me up." (Psalms 71:20)

One of the most common desires of those in recovery is for a "quick-fix". Everyone wants a 1-2-3 plan; all neat and tidy. Over and over we tell everyone there is no such thing. Recovery is a process; a life-long process with successes and lapses. Recovery also isn't a one-size fits all program. Sure, there are some things that need to appear in everyone's recovery but others will be unique to the individual. I have a friend who is a perfectionist so her recovery was made more difficult by wanting to "do it right" and not make any mistakes: Really, an impossible desire. God has a plan for each of us to restore and make us whole. He doesn't want any of us destroyed by traumas in our lives. He wants to use them to strengthen us and our faith. We can trust Him to walk alongside us and show us each step of our process. He sees our troubles, our pain, and our need to recover. He doesn't just turn away and ignore us: We are the *"apple of His eye."*

"'For I know the plans I have for you,' says the Lord, 'plans to prosper you and not to harm you, plans to give you hope and a future.'"
(Jeremiah 29:11)

NOTES:

FORGIVENESS

"For if you forgive men when they sin against you, your heavenly Father will also forgive you." (Matthew 6:14)

Forgiveness falls into three categories: forgiveness from God, forgiveness we give to others, and the ability to forgive ourselves. We struggle with being able to forgive the one who hurt us so badly, ("I will *never* forgive him for what he did to me.") The lack of forgiveness allows bitterness to take hold in the soul. Resentment grows and eventually the original event needing forgiveness becomes larger than life and much harder to forgive. Forgiveness frees us from that bitterness. Forgiving someone for how they wounded you does not mean that you ever have to have a relationship with that person again, nor does it mean that everything is back to normal, as if nothing had ever happened. Lack of forgiveness is a burden God never meant for us to carry; it is just too heavy. Forgiveness is an act of the will; it's not a feeling. It doesn't make you feel all warm and fuzzy. It's a process that occurs over time and happens again and again. It's not a "happily ever after" act that magically sets all things right. It took me a long time before I realized that in spite of what my husband had done, I too, was a sinner needing forgiveness. In God's eyes the ground in front of the cross is level.

"Who can discern his errors? Forgive my hidden faults." (Psalms 19:12)

NOTES:

JUST GET OVER IT

"Now I urge you to take some food. You need it to survive. Not one of you will lose a single hair from his head." (Acts 27:34)

In Kings 18 and 19 we read an amazing story of Elijah, his victory over 450 prophets of Baal, and the results of that event. Elijah experienced depression and felt alone and abandoned, like he was the only prophet of God left. He was in a fragile emotional condition and God took him through a process of recovery. One of the most damaging things someone may say to you is that you should just "get over it." To be told to "get over it" implies that whatever you have been or are hurting about isn't important enough for you to continue thinking about. God didn't tell Elijah to "get over it" but ministered to him in practical ways. Many people are ill-equipped to be around others who are in pain and what they want most is for that person to be happy again so they, themselves, won't feel awkward and helpless. There are things that one shouldn't just attempt to "get over" but need to be worked through, grieved, and healed. Allow healing to take place regardless of the time involved. No matter what someone else thinks, the timing of recovery is specific to the individual and should not be rushed but supported and encouraged. God is patient with our recovery and just asks that He be allowed to be our Guide through it.

"Be completely humble and gentle; be patient; bearing with one another in love." (Ephesians 4:2)

DON'T GIVE UP

"But as for you, be strong and do not give up, for your work will be rewarded."(II Chronicles15:7)

When the pain of a loss or wound is great there is sometimes a desire to just give up and quit the work necessary to experience healing. The road just seems too long and the end never in sight. The times when one can say there has been some progress seem to be few and far apart. The tears continue to come at unexpected moments and the temptation is strong to get off the road to recovery. In our bewildered and wounded condition, our thinking is unclear and that is why it is so important to be walking with someone who can be trusted to help make decisions. We need a companion who can talk us through those times when giving up seems to be the most sensible thing to do. The Holy Spirit is the One who can provide the comfort we need. He is called the Comforter, the Counselor, and is always there for us.

"And I will ask the Father, and He will give you another Counselor to be with you forever." (John 14:16)

NOTES:

SUFFICIENT FOR YOU

"And God is able to make all grace abound to you, so that in all things at all times, having all that you need, you will abound in every good work." (II Corinthians 9:8)

In recovery, we find ourselves helpless and powerless in the face of great pain. We have two choices: we can ignore the pain and attempt to escape it or, we can go through a healing process that takes time and effort. The way we can most effectively do the latter is to accept the grace of God; to admit that we are powerless and must have help outside ourselves. God's grace is defined as His "unmerited, undeserved favor" and is freely given. There is nothing we can do to earn it or deserve it and it is unlimited. God's grace is like a huge, soft pillow that we can fall into; a place of comfort and safety where our wounds are eased for a while. To be able to release the need to control our circumstances (which we can't do anyway) is an immense relief but very difficult in our "I can do it myself" society. Run to that safe place that God offers. It's free!

"But He said to me, 'My grace is sufficient for you, for my power is made perfect in weakness.'" (II Corinthians 12:9)

NOTES:

ATTITUDE OF GRATITUDE

"Let the word of Christ dwell in you richly as you teach and admonish one another with all wisdom, and as you sing psalms, hymns and spiritual songs with gratitude in your hearts to God." (Colossians 3:16)

In the early stages of recovery, it is hard to find anything to be grateful for. Where there was color, now there is only a gray, dingy coating. Things that caused happiness, humor, or joy are replaced with sadness, confusion, and sometimes depression. This is the time when we must push on regardless of how we feel because hope tells us that on the other side of gloom and despair is life once again. We need not always be in a place of darkness but can come out on the other side of the storm even stronger than before. During this time of sadness we have to make an effort to find something, anything to be grateful for because this can lift us even momentarily out of being so focused on our pain. Being thankful for your children's health, the first daffodil of spring, the goofy way your dog plays with her favorite toy helps us to have respite from the pain and to look for just an instant into the face of the One who can heal our pain and who deserves our gratitude.

"The Lord is my Strength and my Shield; my heart trusts in Him, and I am helped. My heart leaps for joy and I will give thanks to Him in song." (Psalms 28:7)

NOTES:

NO PAIN, NO GAIN

"Heal me, O Lord, and I will be healed; save me and I will be saved, for You are the One I praise."(Jeremiah 17:14)

"No pain, no gain." This is a statement we hear many times in reference to the training of athletes as they stretch and push their muscles to do what they resist doing. In the process there is a strengthening that would not come in any other way. The goal of the recovery process is to create health and wholeness in broken people. Hearts that are already broken are pushed to new limits in order to achieve that goal. In our healing process there are times when we feel we are being broken all over again and we cry out to God, but He continues pushing because He sees the bigger picture of our eventual healing. He knows that the pain we will go through will be worth the healing we will experience. Only after we have achieved a degree of wholeness, however, are we able to look back and see where we've come from and even appreciate it.

"But we have this treasure in jars of clay to show that this all-surpassing power is from God and not from us. We are hard pressed on every side, but not crushed, perplexed, but not in despair; persecuted, but not abandoned, struck down, but not destroyed."(II Corinthians 4:7-9)

NOTES:

A BROKEN HEART

"....so the king asked me, 'Why does your face look so sad when you are not ill? This can be nothing but sadness of heart.' I was very much afraid." (Nehemiah 2:2)

The only way we can even partially understand a broken heart is to have had one ourselves. Even when the causes are not the same we can still say, "I'm so sorry" and really mean it. Many things can cause a broken heart and they all have to do with relationships that have been damaged in some way. Heartbreak causes pain; sometimes from others, sometimes from things that we have done. This can be illustrated by a cracked or broken vase. We can use the best glue available, sometimes even having it repaired professionally, but the crack is still there. It may not be visible any longer but the scar always remains and under scrutiny can be seen. Despite how it feels right now, broken hearts can mend; it just takes time and the willingness to go through grieving process. Healing *is* on the other side. Life won't "go back to normal" because the scars of a broken heart are there to remind us of our losses. Even scars fade though, and can be reminders for us of God's healing power.

"The cords of death entangled me, the anguish of the grace came upon me; I was overcome by trouble and sorrow. Then I called on the name of the Lord: 'O Lord, save me.' The Lord is gracious and righteous; our God is full of compassion." (Psalms116:3)

NOTES:

HELPLESSNESS

"When He saw the crowds, He had compassion on them, because they were harassed and helpless, like sheep without a shepherd."(Matthew 9:36)

It is very uncomfortable, even disconcerting, to suddenly feel helpless in the face of circumstances which you cannot control. If you have been able to manage in the past and then come up against something out of your realm of experience, it would be likely that you would feel helpless at least for a time. To be thrust into a recovery program because of an unfaithful or addicted spouse would put one in that category. It is not anything you did that caused you to be in the situation and there is nothing you can do to change it. That's certainly a recipe for helplessness. It is appropriate at these times to seek wise counsel from someone with a recovery background. They can help us think "outside the box" which is a necessary tool in combating this. All other avenues of response are closed so our thinking needs to be creative. Sometimes the answers aren't big and flashy but ones that can help us feel a lessening of that confining feeling. Moving ahead through helplessness is stretching for us and necessary for our growth and personal recovery.

"He who walks with the wise grows wise, but a companion of fools suffers harm." (Proverbs 13:20)

NOTES:

HOPE

"Though He slay me, yet will I hope in Him; I will surely defend my ways to His face." (Job.13:15)

Hope enables us to look out of the darkness of our present into the light of the future. It gives us courage to keep going on and desiring that light. Without hope, there seems to be no reason to look ahead any farther than the next minute, and even that doesn't seem to matter. If all we can see or imagine as we look into our future is more pain, disappointment, betrayal, or loss, our life looks pretty bleak. Without true hope, God seems distant and the current situation may seem like punishment from Him. Hopelessness comes from depending on ourselves for all the answers instead of the God who actually **has** those answers and is more than willing to share them with us. When we rely on our own strength and power to move through life, we will more than likely at some point come up against something that we will not be able to control. God wants us to look to Him for our hope because real hope doesn't come from what we will be able to accomplish in the future or how famous or rich we will be. Real hope comes from knowing the God of hope and understanding in our limited way that the real future is not here, not now, but in eternity with the God who will guide us through this life; the only true source of hope.

"Do not let your hearts be troubled. Trust in God; trust also in Me." (John 14:1)

HURTING EACH OTHER

"Love is patient....It always protects, always trusts, always hopes, always perseveres. Love never fails." (I Corinthians 13:4-7)

There are many ways we can be hurt. It can be physical, emotional, or spiritual, but it always comes from other people. Some wounds are visible while others are buried deeply and never discussed. We hurt each other unintentionally with a hasty or unkind word. Relationships within families are probably the most vulnerable to hurt because of our close bonds, blood ties. Those closest to us have the ability to hurt us the most. Knowledge of that is vital in avoiding some of the hurt because we don't want to hurt someone we love. To be hurt deeply by someone you have loved is a pain that is not easily healed and will often leave an emotional scar. Being hurt can also cause new caution, a lack of trust, or being skeptical. If we weren't all capable of hurting each other, there would be no need for us to be reminded over and over in the Bible to be kind to each other. After all, God knows people. He created us and we're challenged to look to Him for ways to avoid hurting each other.

"Be kind and compassionate to one another, forgiving each other, just as in Christ God forgave you." (Ephesians 4:32)

NOTES:

BE ALERT!

"Search me, O God, and know my heart; test me and know my anxious thoughts." (Psalms 139:23)

Women are blessed with what is called "women's intuition". We get feelings that seem to have no basis in hard evidence. It may just be a feeling of uneasiness or alarm. When this happens I believe there needs to be some investigation done in determining what is causing the feeling. We don't feel "ill at ease" with no reason. Something inside is telling us to beware; there is reason to be anxious or questioning. Don't ignore these feelings but be more attentive to other signs that there are things wrong. Don't deny but take action. Don't let fear of what you may find out stop you from learning the truth. When something does happen, you may look back and remember that you "had a feeling". Pay attention. God has given us the Holy Spirit who has promised to "lead us into all truth" and give us guidance beyond ourselves. Being "awake" and alert is an important part of your recovery.

"So, then, let us not be like others, who are asleep, but let us be alert and self-controlled."(I Thessalonians 5:6)

NOTES:

DON'T BELIEVE IT

"How long, O Lord? Will You forget me forever? How long will You hide Your face from me? How long must I wrestle with my thoughts and everyday have sorrow in my heart? (Psalms 13:1-2)

Some people say that Christians should never be depressed. For these people, depression would signal a lack of trust or some sin in your life that you've not repented of. They say that if God, by way of the Holy Spirit, was **really** living in you, you would not be depressed but always joyful, never succumbing to "unhealthy" emotions. The truth is we're just as vulnerable to breakdowns in our minds and bodies as anyone else. Don't let anyone tell you differently. That lie has kept a lot of Christians from seeking the help they so desperately need. What separates us from non-Christians is the resource of our God who knows just how to bring healing into our lives. King David experienced depression and the Psalms are full of his declarations of grief, sorrow, and loss. His emotional state lasted for years through adultery, murder, betrayal, and attempts on his life. Through all of his desperate times though, there is a sense of him holding tightly onto the rope that tied him to his God. Sometimes it seemed like God wasn't there at all but, David's cry is always a cry of the heart; a heart after God, a man after God's own heart." (excerpt from "Making a Quilt Out of Cobwebs")

"Be merciful to me, O Lord, for I am in distress; my eyes grow weak with sorrow, my soul and my body with grief. My life is consumed by anguish and my years by groaning; my strength fails because of my affliction, and my bones grow weak. But I trust in You, O Lord. I say, 'You are my God.'" (Psalms 31:9-10)

BE PATIENT

"Love is patient, love is kind. It does not envy, it does not boast, it is not proud."(I Corinthians 13:4)

When a couple is involved in the recovery process, they must understand that those processes will be different for each of them. The addict will feel great relief and freedom after his disclosure, while the opposite happens for the wife. She receives a huge, unwanted burden and more pain than she could imagine. Because of this disparity, the addict can sometimes become impatient with his wife's progress. She will seem far behind him in her recovery and it may take longer for her than for him. This is a reality because the pain and shame he has shed have become hers. What she will experience as a result, will be far different than what he goes through. An addict doesn't want to see his wife's pain because he is reminded that it's because of him that she feels it. He wants her to 'move on' and not make him feel badly by seeing her hurting. If he is a smart man he will keep all that impatience to himself and understand that, after all, if it weren't for him, she wouldn't need to recover at all. A wife deserves respect and the time to recover fully. Impatience will only make things worse instead of moving things along.

"A patient man has great understanding, but a quick-tempered man displays folly." (Proverbs 14:29)

NOTES:

KNOWING YOU

"A man of many companions may come to ruin, but there is a friend who sticks closer than a brother." (Proverbs 18:14)

When we hear the word "intimacy" most of us automatically think of the sexual or physical relationship. Real intimacy is so much more. Intimacy demands that a person be emotionally involved and known on a deeper level by another. Intimacy enables a couple to see each other across a room and, knowing the other's thoughts, smile. True intimacy gives a couple strength to stand against a society that devalues marriage and encourages jumping from one bed to another; to 'know' as well as 'be known' and loved in spite of our warts. It is a bond formed when there is trust and communication at a depth not shared with others. God desires an intimacy with us that requires more than just head knowledge of Him but a trust and love for Him that is unshakeable in the crises of life.

"Before a word in on my tongue, You know it completely, O Lord. You hem me in, behind and before; You have laid Your hand upon me. Such knowledge is too wonderful for me, too lofty for me to attain." (Psalms 139:4-6)

NOTES:

GRIEVING THE LOSSES

"What is more, I consider everything a loss compared to the surpassing greatness of knowing Christ Jesus my Lord, for whose sake I have lost all things. I consider them rubbish that I may gain Christ."
(Philippians 3:8)

One of the most important things I had to do during my recovery process was admit and then record the losses I had incurred as a result of my husband's addiction. Admitting those losses causes them to become more real and, being real, can be grieved. At first I couldn't really think of any 'real' losses but I was part of a women's group and hearing from the other women helped me identify some. It wasn't long before I had written down almost two pages of losses. Understanding that I had incurred losses validated my pain. There was no denial left and the grieving process could begin. The pain that I had felt suddenly had a name and I began to be able to work through it rather than feeling like I was trying to catch smoke.

"Yet I am always with You; You hold me by my right hand. You guide me with Your counsel, and afterward You will take me into glory. My flesh and my heart may fail, but God is the strength of my heart and my portion forever." (Psalms 73:23-24, 26)

NOTES:

LOVE IS.....

"For God so loved the world that He gave His only begotten Son that whosoever believes in Him shall not perish but have everlasting life." (John 3:16)

Love between two people has lost its' real meaning and instead become synonymous with sexual attraction and romance. Many people don't even think about loving someone as being emotionally intimate with them or having any long term commitment. They live together before marriage with the idea that "if it doesn't work out" they won't have been tied down by legal documents. Even those who get married professing to love one another, walk away in droves as soon as the sexual ardor or romance wanes. "Till death do us part" are only words uttered as part of the pageantry of the marriage ceremony. Many are married today without being prepared in any way for the work of keeping a marriage alive and vital. Love is so much more than what we see on television. Love is a commitment to each other that lasts through the hard times as well as the good times. It's a determination to stand together against what the world throws at you. Love is about the other person; not about you. Love is sacrificial; thinking about the needs of the one loved. God is Love. He is our example.

"But God demonstrates His own love for us in this: While we were still sinners, Christ died for us." (Romans 5:8)

NOTES:

JUMPY?

"An anxious heart weighs a man down, but a kind word cheers him up." (Proverbs 12:25)

When your place of security is shaken to the core, it is only natural to feel insecure or anxious for a time. To be nervous and jumpy all the time can signal a deeper emotional trauma that needs to be worked out with a counselor or your physician. There was a time several years ago when I was in that state. It didn't come on me suddenly but over a period of a couple of years so that I didn't notice how I had deteriorated emotionally. The people closest to me did though and gently suggested counseling. I resisted that for a time but eventually began weekly counseling. I went from being highly agitated and paranoid to calm and able, once again, to deal with life on a daily basis. God shows His mercy and love for us by providing us with professionals able to guide us through the dark valleys. He never expects us to go alone.

"When anxiety was great within me, Your consolation brought joy to my soul." (Psalms 94:19)

"Cast all your anxiety on Him because He cares for you." (I Peter 5:7)

NOTES:

BACK TO NORMAL

"Jesus Christ is the same yesterday and today and forever." (Hebrews 13:8)

The thing that I wished for the most after my husband's disclosure of sexual addiction was that everything would be back to "normal". That seemed to be a safe place, back there in "normal" land. Before disclosure, I was secure and things were going smoothly. After, my world fell apart and as much as I wished for it, there was no going back. I finally realized (over time) that there was no such place as "normal" and certainly no getting back there. I had to allow God to lead me into a new "normal" place where things weren't terrifying and strange anymore; a place where He had control and I didn't need to be afraid." The best "normal" place we can be is in the palm of God's hand. That never changes.

"Every good and perfect gift is from above, coming down from the Father of the heavenly lights, who does not change like shifting shadows." (James 1:17)

NOTES:

BEEN THERE, DONE THAT

"...known, yet regarded as unknown, dying, and yet we live on; beaten, and yet not killed." (II Corinthians 6:9)

The feelings that can and do sweep over a person who has been betrayed are generally overwhelming in their scope and intensity. It feels as though a tidal wave has swept over and you're tossed around like a tiny piece of wood. After that wave subsides, you're left lying bruised and shaken; barely able to catch your breath. In the normal course of recovery, that feeling of being overwhelmed fades and we are gradually able to handle life again. I imagine Jesus felt nearly overwhelmed when He was praying in the Garden of Gethsemane. The emotions He was experiencing were so intense that as He grappled with them, He sweat blood. The struggle to give up His will in submission to His Father's was incredibly difficult and yet, with God's help, He was able to be obedient. As the crowd coming to arrest Him surged forward, He knew betrayal and pain such as we will never experience. Yet, we are assured that whatever we go through, He understands because He has already been there, done that. We can be comforted remembering that we are not alone.

"During the days of Jesus' life on earth, He offered up prayers and petitions with loud cries and tears to the One who could save Him from death, and He was heard because of His reverent submission." (Hebrews 5:7)

NOTES:

PAIN

"I am in pain and distress; may your salvation, O God, protect me."
*Psalms 69:29)

"Take two aspirin and call me in the morning" is a saying that we think of when we have a headache. Any kind of pain, no matter what the degree sends us running to the medicine cabinet for a remedy. The pain of betrayal is much harder to treat. It's not the same as a scraped knee or a broken arm. The wounds are deep and not very visible unless one happens to see the tears that flow without warning. While we try to find remedies for this pain, there aren't many that will make us feel better. Through prayer and crying out in pain to our Heavenly Father, God can bring soothing, healing grace to battered emotions. True healing takes time and effort. Just at the time we feel the weakest, we have to be determined to pursue the wholeness God wants for us. This is the only true remedy for the pain of a broken heart.

"My grace is sufficient for you, for my power is made perfect in weakness." (II Corinthians 12:9)
NOTES:

FROZEN

"Since they could not get him to Jesus because of the crowd, they made an opening in the roof above Jesus and, after digging through it, lowered the mat the paralyzed man was lying on." (Matthew 2:4)

When we are thrust unexpectedly into an unfamiliar, frightening place we can become paralyzed by our emotions and there are so many bombarding us that we can't sort them out to understand what is happening to us. Fear is a great paralyzer; the old "deer in the headlights" syndrome. Something is coming right at you and you are frozen in place staring into the face of great pain. Courage is defined as "action in the face of fear." To think we should never be afraid is unreasonable because we are human, finite; we are made of "dust". When we take just one small step away from our fear and being paralyzed by it, we begin to overcome it. God wants us to never lose sight of the fact that He is right beside us every step and there is nothing that He can't protect us from. He's never afraid!

"A man's steps are directed by the Lord. How then can anyone understand his own way?" (Proverbs .20:24)

NOTES:

911

"Many are the foes who persecute me, but I have not turned from Your statues." (Psalms 119:157)

One of the possible symptoms of severe depression is becoming paranoid. People are looking at me or they're talking about me, among others. Our minds are so busy trying to protect us from any more pain that they begin to see pain, or the possibility of it, everywhere, even in the most innocent of places or people. Over a period of a couple of years I descended slowly into severe depression, sleeplessness, and anxiety with paranoia. If I was home alone at night I had various escape routes planned out just in case someone broke into the house. I didn't think it was unusual that I had the phone in my hand to call 911 or I would break into a sweat if a car rolled slowly by our house. I finally heard God's still, small voice directing me to call a counselor which I did. God has so many methods of bringing healing and deliverance but many times He uses processes that we need to go through in order to restore us to health; to bring us back from a place of darkness. God has a plan for each one of us and our challenge is to open our eyes and see the road ahead.

" 'You will seek me and find me when you seek me with all your heart. I will be found by you,' declares the Lord, 'and will bring you back from captivity.'" (Jeremiah 29:13-14)

NOTES:

NOT IN A HURRY

"The end of a matter is better than its beginning, and patience is better than pride."(Ecclesiastes 7:8)

There is no "quick fix" in recovery. I'd be a zillionaire if I could come up with one, patent it, and sell it. Unfortunately it takes work and lots of patience. We can be very impatient with ourselves or our spouse when the progress isn't as fast as we would like it to be. A lot of times our goal is to get past the pain instead of working through it and recovering thoroughly. It's generally in retrospect that we can see progress. Writing in a journal allows us to look back and see how far we've come. Being patient is part of loving yourself. Don't put any more pressure on yourself by being impatient with your progress. Patience is hard enough when we have to use it on others but on ourselves, it's almost unheard of. There is a part of our humanity that drives us unreasonably, that causes us to have expectations of our own abilities that are unrealistic. Patience during recovery is like a muscle that has to be exercised all the time or it atrophies and we can't use it. God is never in a hurry or impatient with us; we can be gentle with ourselves.

"Yet I am always with You; You hold me by my right hand. You guide me with Your counsel, and afterward, You will take me into glory." (Psalms 73:23-24)

NOTES:

HIS PEACE

"Do not be anxious about anything....and the peace of God, which transcends all understanding, will guard your hearts and your minds in Christ Jesus."(Philippians 4:6-7)

The peace that this verse is talking about is one that we cannot conjure up by ourselves. It is a peace from God that guards your heart and your mind against attacks from the very things that cause us the most unrest: discouragement, anxiety, fear, and loss of hope to name a few. We can't understand this peace because it is nothing found here on earth; it goes beyond our understanding. It is the peace of God and try as we may, we can't create it. It is what allows you to feel calm in the midst of the storm of emotional trauma. I heard a saying several years ago that I think of often: "God won't take the child out of the storm but He will take the storm out of the child." God wants us to depend on Him to see us through any storm and the more we trust Him to do that, the more peace we will experience. It won't come from any other source.

"Peace I leave with you; my peace I give you. I do not give to you as the world gives. Do not let your hearts be troubled and do not be afraid." (John 14:27)

NOTES:

RUN THE RACE

"You need to persevere so that when you have done the will of God, you will receive what He has promised." (Hebrews 10:36)

Perseverance is defined as "continued, patient effort." It's not the supreme effort of running a 100 yard dash but the slow, steady pace of a marathon. It's so tempting to give up and curl up when the pain is intense and we can't seem to rise above it. Many times our progress isn't measurable and we're tempted to lose heart. Stay on course! Sometimes the only progress we see for a while is getting up every day and putting one foot in front of the other. Good job! Sometimes, that's all we're capable of, but if we persevere we will find our muscles getting stronger. At times we want to run as far and as fast as possible to try to escape the inescapable. Recovery has its hills and valleys and mostly it seems like the valleys are far deeper than the hills are higher, but we push on through that pain. We heard recently that "the worst thing you can do when you're going through hell is to stop." Perseverance, that determined patient effort, will help you move on through those valleys, through "hell". We're encouraged to "press on."

"Forgetting what is behind and straining toward what is ahead, I press on toward the goal to win the prize for which God has called me heavenward in Christ Jesus." (Philippians 3:13-14)

NOTES:

BE STILL

"The Lord your God is with you, He is mighty to save. He will take great delight in you, He will quiet you with His love, He will rejoice over you with singing." (Zephaniah 3:17)

When we are in the grip of emotional trauma and the pain associated with it, there seems to be a marked absence of "quiet" voices in our heads. Our battered emotions clamor to be heard, each shouting louder than the last. "Quiet" is something we long for, but don't know how to attain at this point. Part of the problem is that we've never really learned how to be quiet; to just sit in silence. It feels awkward and uncomfortable to just sit alone with God. We feel like we have to fill the silence with talking or music. We just can't stand the "quiet". Be assured that the only place you will really find the "quiet" that you need right now is in the arms of God. Our verse says, *"He will quiet you with His love..."* and as you practice letting God comfort you, you will experience the "quiet" that your wounded heart longs for. You will find a soothing ointment bringing the beginnings of healing.

"Be still and know that I am God; I will be exalted among the nations, I will be exalted in the earth." (Psalms 46:10)

NOTES:

THE WHOLE TRUTH

"For the word of the Lord is right and true; He is faithful in all He does." (Psalms 33:4)

When your emotional world comes tumbling down around you, it's normal to think "If the one I love the most lies to me, who doesn't?" It seems as if suddenly what was real and solid becomes like fog that blows away and can't be caught. Everyone around you becomes suspect; their words and motives take on new and sometimes sinister meanings. Even our own feelings and ability to think clearly and be logical come into question. We think we've been made fools of and that somehow it is our fault. To be able to recognize the truth vs. the lie becomes very important because our enemy wants us to believe the lie and remain in pain and confusion, trusting no one. A good friend of mine taught me to ask myself "What is true about this situation (these words, this feeling, etc.)?" That causes me to think rather than just react. It also gives the Holy Spirit an opportunity to speak peace into my heart when I come across the truth.

"Send forth Your light and Your truth, let them guide me; let them bring me to Your holy mountain, to the place where you dwell." (Psalms 43:3)

"Teach me Your way, O Lord, and I will walk in Your truth; give me an undivided heart, that I may fear Your name." (Psalms 86:11)

NOTES:

IT TAKES TWO

"I am not saying this because I am in need, for I have learned to be content whatever the circumstances." (Philippians 4:11)

Maybe the most important thing I've learned about reconciliation is that is starts with my relationship with God. If I am in right relationship with Him, I am more likely to be able to make wise decisions in other situations. My perspective is different, coming from a spiritual standpoint rather than a fleshly one. I think most of us want to reconcile with our husbands/partners when there is a betrayal, but it's not always possible. Sadly, too often only one half of the couple is really interested in doing whatever it takes to be reconciled. Yes, God "hates" divorce but we don't always listen and become more and more determined to go our own ways. To "reconcile" requires two people who are "submissive or acquiescent" to **each other**, a mutual respect and honoring of one another. In our relationship with God, He always desires reconciliation and He did what it took to make it possible: the death of His Son.

"Once you were alienated from God and were sinners in your minds because of your evil behavior. But now He has reconciled you by Christ's physical body through death to present you holy in His sight, without blemish and free from accusation." (Colossians 1:21-22)

NOTES:

IT'S A PROCESS

"Again I ask: Did they stumble so as to fall beyond recovery?"
(Romans 11:11)

Recovery is defined as "a regaining of something lost or stolen; a return to health, consciousness; a regaining of balance, control, composure." This definition implies a moving away from a healthy position to an unhealthy one. In "recovery" we're moving toward a healthier place and one where we're able to experience balance and composure in our lives once again. Recovery is definitely a process just as there is a safe and optimum method of climbing a mountain. In climbing, you don't get to start at ground level then suddenly find yourself on the mountaintop: no effort, no discomfort, and no challenge along the way. It's the same with the recovery mountain. We start where we are and move along the path that God lays out for us. He has planned out a route and there will be effort, challenge, and some discomfort, but He will give us the strength we need for every step of the climb.

"Therefore, since we are surrounded by such a great cloud of witnesses, let us throw off everything that hinders and the sin that so easily entangles, and let us run with perseverance the race marked out for us." (Hebrews 12:1)
NOTES:

A NEW PLACE

"Restore to me the joy of Your salvation and grant me a willing spirit to sustain me." (Psalms 51:12)

There are many things that are lost or taken away when there is a breakdown in relationships caused by betrayal or addiction. To "restore" implies taking a relationship back to its former condition or place. In reality, from a recovery standpoint, going back to a former place is not the desired goal. The former place was a place of pain, betrayal, and loss. We want a new relationship based on truth, trust, and healthy emotions. There may be some pieces of the old relationship that can be salvaged, for example, years spent together as best friends, or raising of children but, for the most part, there is a need to start over with a new foundation, not just restore the old one. The Bible has several things to say about going from an "old life" to a "new life" and that is what we want for our marriages. We all know where we've come from. Let God show you where you're going.

"You were taught, with regard to your former way of life, to put off your old self, which is being corrupted by its deceitful desires ; to be made new in the attitude of your minds; and to put on the new self, created to be like God in true righteousness and holiness."(Ephesians 4:22)

NOTES:

OUR REFUGE

"For in the day of trouble He will keep me safe in His dwelling, He will hide me in the shelter of His tabernacle and set me high upon a rock."
(Psalms 27:5)

The loss of safety and security is felt deeply when there is a betrayal. There is a definite sense of the rug being pulled out from under you. Feeling "unsafe" is very real and there are things that can be done to ease it. Establishing boundaries is an excellent way to begin to have a sense of safety once again. Within those boundaries, you are safe and feel some confidence. Outside, the unknown world crowds around and makes you feel vulnerable again. Unfortunately, it's necessary to make a distinction between "safe" and "unsafe" people. Some people simply can't be trusted to validate your feelings or keep your confidences: they just don't know how. They aren't equipped to deal with the pain they see in you and aren't mature enough to know what to say or how to act around you. A "safe" person is one of the same sex who listens, is trustworthy, supportive, and keeps confidences. You need to have some people to walk with you through this traumatic time and should seek out those people. Don't hurry though, and pray for discernment to know who God has in mind for you. At the end of the day, though, there is only one safe place, one safe Person, and that is our Heavenly Father.

"In the shelter of Your presence You hide them from the intrigues of men; in Your dwelling You keep them safe from the strife of tongues."
(Psalms 31:20)

IN THE RIGHT HANDS

"He may let them rest in a feeling of security, but His eyes are on their ways." (Job 24:23)

"Don't put all your eggs in one basket" is a phrase I've heard since I was a child. It means that if you do and then you drop the basket, all the eggs will be broken. It refers to putting all your hopes, all your trust, all your security in one person; one fallible, human person. By doing that, we set ourselves up for hurt and disappointment. God is the only One worthy of all our hope, trust, and security. As vulnerable human beings, we will all hurt one another at one time or another; it's a given. We won't necessarily mean to and it won't always be malicious but it will happen. Our security will likely be destroyed or at least severely shaken if it is in the hands of one man or one woman and most certainly if there is a betrayal in the relationship. It isn't wise or safe to entrust your security to someone else. Of course, there needs to be a *level* of security (trust) in a marriage but the greater weight should be placed in God's hands. Balance it between the abilities of man vs. the abilities of God.

"Nevertheless, I will bring health and healing to it; I will heal My people and will let them enjoy abundant peace and security." (Jeremiah 33:6)

NOTES:

SHAME OFF YOU

"No one whose hope is in You will ever be put to shame, but they will be put to shame who are treacherous without excuse." (Psalms 25:3)

Shame is one of the most powerful emotions a person can feel and has the ability to keep one locked in patterns of behavior that even they find wretched. While guilt is felt in response to something a person has **done**, shame is a feeling about who a person **is** and the value/worth of that person. To live in shame is like having strong chains wrapped around you that you can't break free of. The only way to be freed from those chains is to understand your worth in God's eyes. The Holy Spirit brings conviction when we sin but God never shames us: We're too precious to Him for Him to make us question our value and worth. Our place in His family is one that He planned before the creation of the world.

"Long ago, even before He made the world, God loved us and chose us in Christ to be holy and without fault in His eyes. His unchanging plan has always been to adopt us into His own family by bringing us to Himself through Jesus Christ. And this gave Him great pleasure." (Ephesians.1:4-5) (NLT)

"But God demonstrates His own love for us in this" While we were still sinners, Christ died for us."(Romans 5:8)

NOTES:

NOT BY MIGHT

"My flesh and my heart may fail, but God is the strength of my heart and my portion forever." (Psalms 73:26)

Pain has the ability to drain all of our emotional resources away and make us feel helpless and powerless. We feel weak and unable to move much or make decisions. The verse in Psalms clearly states that our condition may *feel* hopeless but God has not left us and continues to be the strength we need. He really is the only One who can pull you through the swamp of pain to the solid ground of recovery. He will give you the strength you need to put one foot in front of the other and to continue following Him along the path that leads to health once again.

"The Lord is my strength and my shield; my heart trusts in Him, and I am helped. My heart leaps for joy and I will give thanks to Him in song." (Psalms.28:7)

NOTES:

TEARS IN A BOTTLE

"I am worn out from groaning; all night long I flood my bed with weeping and drench my couch with tears." (Psalms 6:5)

In the beginning of my recovery process I didn't want to cry. I was afraid that if I got started I wouldn't be able to stop. When I did cry there were plenty of times that it took the form of gut-wrenching sobbing, but each time I did eventually stop. There were just enough tears for that one session it seems. I learned that crying is a very important part of healing. God gives us tears to help cleanse our hearts of the hurt and pain and I did find that I felt a little bit of relief after a good cry. It is like the lake gets full and the dam overflows until the water level is below the top of the dam. Tears are a part of grieving and very natural. People around you may not understand your tears but that doesn't matter. They are yours and God gave them to you.

"You keep track of all my sorrows. You have collected all my tears in Your bottle. You have recorded each one in Your book." (Psalms56:8) (NLT)

NOTES:

HEAVY WEIGHT

"When I am afraid, I will trust in You." (Psalms 56:3)

Trust is built in a relationship or marriage over time. Being thoughtful, caring for the other person before yourself, making wise choices are all part of building trust. It is somewhat like building a brick wall: brick by brick, the mortar in between holding them tightly. Actions, reactions, behaviors, and attitudes are the brick in the trust "wall". Time and effort build and betrayal tears down. What can take years to build can take moments to destroy. To rebuild that trust is much harder the second time because there is the added weight of hurt and suspicion pushing against the wall. I wasn't sure that I could ever trust my husband again but over time, God showed me that the issue was really about trusting Him to take care of me. Slowly, I realized that God could handle the weight and responsibility of my trust. It became less important that my husband never failed and more obvious that both of us would.

"Those who know Your name will trust in You, for You, Lord, have never forsaken those who seek You." (Psalms 9:10)

NOTES:

DEEP BREATHS

"The Lord is my Shepherd, I shall lack nothing. He makes me lie down in green pastures, He leads me beside quiet waters, He restores my soul. He guides me in the paths of righteousness for His name's sake." (Psalms 23:1-3)

We all have our own ways to relax. For me, relaxation takes place when I am by myself. When someone else is with you there is usually a feeling that you need to have conversation. Alone, that's only necessary if you're talking to God. The thought of being alone for any length of time may be frightening to some of you. Being comfortable with "alone-time" is something that is learned. In our society we are surrounded by all kinds of noise, commotion, and people. Busyness is a way of life and exhaustion goes hand in hand with it. To be able to really relax can be done in various ways. You may like to take a long bubble bath with soft music and candles. Maybe you relax best when you're at a park sitting on a bench. Not too far from our house, there is a river that has a walking path along side it. Many times I sat on a bench just watching the water go by and listening to the wind in the trees. It was very soothing to let those things just wash over me and relax my mind and heart in quietness for a time.

"In repentance and rest is your salvation, in quietness and trust is your strength, but you would have none of it." (Isaiah 30:15)

NOTES:

FREE TO FEEL

"Surely You desire truth in the inner parts; You teach me wisdom in the inmost place." (Psalms 51:6)

For many of us there is a lot of guilt associated with emotions we feel especially when they are passionate ones. It's almost as if there is an unspoken edict that Christians shouldn't feel deeply in what are considered "negative" ways. God created us with our emotions and Jesus is our example of feeling and using them. Jesus portrayed passionate anger when He found men in the temple area selling animals and exchanging money. (John2:13-17), He asserted His identity as He taught in the temple courts (John 6:28-29) and, He grieved deeply at the death of His friend, Lazarus (John 11:35). Part of our recovery journey is to learn and experience truth and honesty in our emotions, regardless of what other people think. It's another example of how we have to lean on God for strength because we certainly don't have any of our own; particularly when we're going against the established code of behavior. Trust God to show you how to express and work through your emotions. It's part of the healthy life He desires for you. Be free!

"Take off the grave clothes and let him go." (John 11:44)

NOTES:

SHED THE SECOND SKIN

"He forgives all my sins and heals all my diseases." (Psalms 103:3)

God knows that we are not inclined to forgive without His prompting. We are so human; we hold onto our pain and woundedness like a second skin. He knows that the lack of forgiveness is a form of bondage. The layers of pain, bitterness, anger, hatred, and revenge form around us in an impenetrable barrier. They cause us to be hard inside. Forgiveness is about freedom and above all, He wants us to be free from the bonds, the slavery of an unforgiving heart. The Scriptures dealing with forgiveness all seem to speak to the ***forgiver*** about the consequences of an unforgiving heart. Our responsibility is to allow God to cleanse and guard ***our*** hearts and spirits, not the other party's. The benefits of forgiveness are for us, not our offender.

"But when you are praying, first forgive anyone you are holding a grudge against so that your Father in heaven will forgive your sins, too."(Matthew 11:25)

NOTES:

THE GREATEST OF THESE

"When I was a child, I talked like a child, I thought like a child, I reasoned like a child. When I became a man, I put childish ways behind me. Now we see but a poor reflection; then we shall see face to face. Now I know in part; then I shall know fully, even as I am fully known. And now, these three remain: faith, hope and love. But the greatest of these is love." (I Corinthians 13:11-13)

For a long time, I didn't care if I ever loved my husband again. I felt like he had thrown my love away and didn't deserve to be loved. I could give no assurances of a future love. God began to teach me about love and one of the first things was that love chooses to exist. It is not dependent upon feelings, but is not void of them. I couldn't begin to expect to love my husband again unless I chose to do so. Choosing to love again was part of my process of recovery; accepting love as it really is instead of the idealized love of songs. I had no idea how to go about rebuilding what was destroyed. I didn't even know if I wanted to. As I turned that dilemma over to God, the pressure was relieved. It was enough to give God the responsibility of putting our relationship and, eventually, our love back together again.

NOTES:

WORTH MORE THAN SPARROWS

"Are not two sparrows sold for a penny? Yet not one of them will fall to the ground apart from the will of your Father. And even the very hairs of your head are all numbered. So don't be afraid; you are worth more than many sparrows." (Matthew 11:29-31)

One of the most important things that can happen to any of us, man or woman, is to have our feelings validated. That means that they are important, worthy of esteem for their own sake or having intrinsic worth. I would guess that we have all been told at one time or another "Oh, you shouldn't feel *that* way." Well, we do feel *that* way but we push those feelings back because we've been told that they aren't appropriate, aren't worth feeling, or aren't valid. To deny our feelings and their importance requires a deadening of our emotions and the outlet those emotions provide. When we have been betrayed there are so many emotions flying around and we have to deal with them as we are able. Don't allow anyone to tell you that you shouldn't feel a certain way. That's a lie and you have every right to your feelings. God created us with emotion; it's part of our humanity. Your healing depends on addressing and working through the feelings of hurt, rejection, betrayal, abandonment, anger, and more. Your feelings are valid and when someone acknowledges the depth of your hurt, you are validated as a person and enabled to move on through that pain to a place of wholeness.

NOTES:

TAME THE TONGUE

"If the Lord had not been on our side---let Israel say---if the Lord had not been on our side when men attacked us, when their anger flared against us, they would have swallowed us alive; the flood would have engulfed us, the torrent would have swept over us, the raging waters would have swept us away."(Psalms 124:1-2)

In this Psalm, King David is acknowledging his vulnerability without the Lord being on his side, watching over him. He realized his position and understood he was subject to attack. In the same way, our woundedness makes us vulnerable to criticism, being more easily hurt, and being extra sensitive. We're already hurt, and insensitive people come along and make the most amazingly unfortunate remarks. If they stopped and thought about what they were about to say, chances are they wouldn't go on. Seldom are the comments designed to hurt but under the guise of giving what they think is good advice or encouragement, they end up rubbing salt in a wound. Sometimes words aren't necessary; a hug will do. I wasn't ever able to respond quickly to unwanted "encouragement" because of my wounded spirit, so the best thing I could do was to give it to God right away so that it wouldn't lodge itself in my heart like a thorn.

"Reckless words pierce like a sword, but the tongue of the wise brings healing." (Psalms 12:18)

NOTES:

WHAT, ME WORRY?

"Therefore, do not worry about tomorrow, for tomorrow will worry about itself. Each day has enough trouble of its own." (Matthew 6:34)

These verses talk about all of the things that are of concern to us; our lives, what to eat or drink, what to wear; things that suddenly take on an even greater significance when our lives and livelihoods are shaken, maybe permanently. God wants us to have a firm grasp on the fact that He **knows** what we need from the smallest thing to the largest. Nothing escapes His attention. In fact, He reminds us that He created the beauty of the lilies and the grass of the field and that we are more important to Him than they. They are beautiful for a short time, then thrown into the fire. Will He not give us much more than we need in order to live? He contrasts us to the pagans (non-believers) who are consumed with chasing after things that are not worth worrying about. He wants our priority to be seeking first His kingdom and His righteousness--the necessities of our spiritual lives. The things we need for our flesh (our temporary lives) He will supply. He knows our needs---let Him worry about our tomorrows.

"Cast your cares on the Lord and He will sustain you; He will never let the righteous fall." (Psalms 55:22)

NOTES:

REAL FAITH

"Be strong and courageous. Do not be afraid or terrified because of them, for the Lord your God goes with you. He will never leave you or forsake you." (Deuteronomy 31:6)

On the road to recovery, our faith takes on new, deeper meaning. Mine took a real beating because I thought God had abandoned me. I found that my faith had been so superficial that it only functioned if things were going well or the crisis was short-lived. Oh, it could survive little bumps and bruises, things we call "trials" but the big test was upon me, and my faith not only faltered, but was staggering around threatening its own death. I had obviously not been "doing it right" and the guilt over that was huge. It finally dawned on me that the kind of faith I had depended on ME and was contingent upon my feelings, circumstances, how other people were treating me, and my perception of God's fairness, mercy, and love for me. It ebbed and flowed like the ocean tides. The kind of faith that God wants for me is the kind that depends totally on Him! Not just that I trust Him or depend on Him, but that I realize faith is a gift coming completely from God and having practically nothing to do with me. I can do nothing to deserve this gift and it is only one of many God offers me for free."

"...let us draw near to God with a sincere heart in full assurance of faith, having our hearts sprinkled to cleanse us from a guilty conscience and having our bodies washed with pure water." (Hebrews 10:22)

REFINED

"For you did not receive a spirit that makes you a slave again to fear, but you received the Spirit of sonship. And by Him we cry, 'Abba, Father.' The Spirit Himself testifies with our spirit that we are God's children." (Romans 8:15)

When our own personal worlds are torn apart, one thing that we must realize is there is no going back. There is only going ahead into what feels very frightening. For what feels like an eternity, there will not be any apparent progress in cleaning up the mess of your life. We struggle with the reality and unfairness of it thinking, "I didn't do anything to deserve this!" As time goes by, we realize that our protests don't change anything. They are only hindering our progress, keeping us stuck wishing for something that can't be. We are going through the fire of refinement and redefinition. The dross is being separated from the gold. What survives now will be real and not an illusion of our own making. As we take each hesitant step, God whispers, "Will you trust Me, even in this?"

"See, I have refined you, though not as silver; I have tested you in the furnace of affliction." (Isaiah 48:10)

NOTES:

HE KNOWS MY NAME

"Fear not, for I have redeemed you; I have called you by name; you are mine." (Isaiah 43:1)

What could be better than for the Creator of the Universe to know your name? I really need to be known by God as His child; a child protected by a loving Father. He knows my name! I am His! Does He want to be the one we run to when our security is threatened or destroyed? Will He allow anything to destroy me? He has told me that He knows my name and I am His! God's name is powerful and can drive away the darkness that sometimes surrounds us. We have an earthly name and He knows it, but He has a special name for each one of us. **Rev.2:17** says, *"He who has an ear, let him hear what the Spirit says to the churches. To him who overcomes, I will give some of the hidden manna. I will also give him a white stone with a **new name** written on it, known only to him who receives it."* **Rev.3:5** continues, *"He who overcomes will, like them, be dressed in white. **I will never erase his name** from the Book of Life, but will acknowledge his name before my Father and His angels."* Knowing someone's name implies a knowledge of them deeper than the surface; a growing intimacy. This is what God has always wanted from us-- for us to know His name, the power, love, forgiveness, and acceptance there. He knows our names; we are special to Him. He loves us!

NOTES:

WHAT DO YOU WANT?

"When Jesus saw him lying there and learned that he had been in this condition for a long time, He asked him, 'Do you want to get well?'" *(John 5:6)*

In John 5, a story is told of Jesus going to Jerusalem and crossing paths with a man who had been an invalid for 38 years. He asked the man what seems like a silly question. 'Do you want to get well?' Now, obviously, when someone is sick they want to be well. However, sometimes, we get so accustomed to our "illness" that we lose hope of ever being well, or feeling good again. This is a condition that we can find ourselves in when we are recovering from the pain of betrayal. The trauma has a way of draining hope away from our spirits and we don't know how to get well any more, not to mention the energy to pursue health and wholeness. Jesus took the time to stop and ask this man a probing question, making him ask himself, 'Well, do I? And, if so, what do I need to be healed?' Jesus wanted the healing to be the man's desire; enough of a desire that he would do what Jesus told him to do. He asks us the same question, 'Do you want to get well?' He asks because He loves us and wants us to live whole, abundant lives. He doesn't want us to be crippled by our pain and despair. He wants us to "pick up our mats and walk".

"Then Jesus said to him, 'Get up! Pick up your mat and walk.' At once the man was cured; he picked up his mat and walked." (John5:8-9)

NOTES:

NO MATTER WHERE

"When they had rowed three or three and a half miles, they saw Jesus approaching the boat, walking on the water; and they were terrified. But He said to them, 'It is I; don't be afraid.'" *(John 6:19-20)*

Sometimes, the darkness surrounding us feels as though it will never go away; that nothing and no one can get in and we can't get out. In this Bible passage, the disciples had been rowing across a lake (an inland sea) for hours. It was night, the wind had picked up and the water grew rough. They began to be very afraid because Jesus wasn't with them. Their confidence was shaken because the situation seemed out of control. It didn't appear that Jesus was, or could be, concerned about them because He wasn't there. When He appeared before them walking on the water, they were terrified. They had never expected or experienced anything like that in their lives. They had no frame of reference for how Jesus got to them. In the same way, we wonder if Jesus has forgotten us. The darkness has fallen, the wind is blowing hard, and the water is so rough we fear drowning. But, we look up, and there He is, walking on the water toward us; arms outstretched, waiting to gather us in. *"It is I; don't be afraid"* He says, providing us with the comfort and peace we need so desperately. No matter where we are, no matter how dark it is, no matter how desperate the situation seems, He will walk on water to reach us. *"It is I; don't be afraid."*

NOTES:

TOO MUCH NOISE

"My sheep listen to my voice; I know them, and they follow me." (John 10:27)

One of the best analogies Jesus used was that of the Good Shepherd. He knows the names of His flock and cares for each one of them as if they were the only one. The Shepherd is spoken of as one who would lay down His life to protect one of His flock. Confusion, fear, and chaos are so loud that they can cause us to lose our way. We no longer hear our Shepherd's voice. He calls us back to safety, but the noise is too great. We can't hear Him. He doesn't give up, though. The "wolf" has attacked the flock and intends to carry away one of the Shepherd's lambs, but He won't let that happen. He understands how we can feel lost and wounded and can wander away. He will leave the rest of the flock and come to get us, tenderly carrying us in His arms, back to the safety of His fold. He is aware of the danger of the wolves and will protect us. As a little lamb wanders away from the Shepherd, she knows little of what she faces, but He does. His goal is to guard and keep safe; no matter how much noise there is around us.

"He calls His own sheep by name and leads them out. When He has brought out all His own, He goes on ahead of them, and His sheep follow Him because they know His voice."(John 10:3-4)

NOTES:

HOPE NOT WISHES

*"....we who have fled to take hold of the **hope** offered to us may be greatly encouraged. We have this **hope** as an anchor for the soul, firm and secure." (Hebrews 6:18-19)*

Recently, I was in Seattle at a conference for women gathered together for one purpose and that was to hear that there is **hope** for them in their situations. **Hope** can be very elusive at times. When the future looks very dark and the pain of living every day becomes overwhelming, **hope** seems out of reach. Sometimes we get confused by the usage of the word. We hear "I hope it won't snow today" or "I hope those shoes are still on sale."

In those phrases, we hear hope as just another way to say "wish" and wishes are like fog that just fades away, nothing substantial. The **hope** that I want you to think about is a noun (a thing) as opposed to a verb (an action). The **hope** that we're offered by our heavenly Father is solid and won't just dry up like the morning dew when the sun hits it. We can rely on the promises of God from the beginning of time right up to today and into the future. The **hope** we're offered and can depend on is *"an anchor for the soul, firm and secure."* We have this **hope** and can be *"greatly encouraged."* When we are at the lowest point of our lives, **hope** is still there. It doesn't go away just because we are grieving, depressed, anxious, or discouraged. It is still solid, still firm, still real, and still promised.

NOTES:

KNOW JESUS, KNOW PEACE

"Peace I leave with you; my peace I give you. I do not give to you as the world gives. Do not let your hearts be troubled and do not be afraid." (John 14:27)

At times, peace is fleeting, our spirits are troubled, and chaos seems to be the norm. It's seldom what is happening *around* us that is the problem, but what is happening *in* us. In fact, what is going on in our hearts and spirits completely colors what we see with our eyes. The peace that God offers us is only available through Christ and His sacrificial death for us; a peace bought with His blood on the cross. The peace that we have through Jesus is not so much a feeling as a condition, a state of mind and heart. It's available supernaturally, not something we just decide we want to feel. Feelings come and go but the peace of Christ supersedes circumstances and situations while the peace the world offers is based on the unlikely cessation of conflict. The peace that Jesus experienced while on earth enabled Him to follow the long road to Calvary. This is the peace we long for; the peace that keeps us from being "troubled and afraid."

"Therefore, since we have been justified through faith, we have peace with God, through our Lord Jesus Christ." (Romans 5:1)

NOTES:

SOUNDS OF HEAVEN

"The Lord your God is with you, He is mighty to save. He will take great delight in you, He will quiet you with His love, He will rejoice over you with singing." (Zephaniah 3:17)

I can't even remember when I heard the phrase "Music soothes the savage beast." Even though I've said it I hadn't given any serious thought to what it meant. I have always loved to sing but many times never really listened to the words. It was only when I was listening with the ears of a broken heart that I heard the words of the praise songs being sung. At first the melodies were soothing and calming, but I eventually started paying attention to the words and found that many of the people who were writing and singing had experienced pain in their own lives. As I let the music sweep over me, I felt peace, even through the tears. When I couldn't read the Bible and felt like God had abandoned me, He loved me through music. The words I heard and sang along with told me I wasn't alone in my pain; that others had been there, too. God, Himself had been there and had already provided comfort for me. God has made Himself known in many ways, and the music of heaven is one of those. Be comforted and refreshed by this provision by your loving Heavenly Father, the Great Composer.

"My heart is steadfast, O God; I will sing and make music with all my soul." (Psalms 108:1)

NOTES:

FIND YOUR REST

"When I said, 'My foot is slipping,' Your love, O Lord, supported me. When anxiety was great within me, Your consolation brought joy to my soul." (Psalms 94:18-19)

When your husband has betrayed you there is such an emotional shock to your system that reasoning and logical actions can get lost in the confusion and chaos. We get so wrapped up in the pain that it seems as if that is all there is and we don't even know how to look for more. Everything in our world causes more of a drain on our fragile energy account and there doesn't seem to be anyplace to get more. No one but God can give the strength that is needed to carry on. He alone can give us rest for a few precious moments at a time. It takes real determination to move even a little ways away from your pain to a place where you can take hold of His rest for a time. In order to function, in some of the really important areas of our lives, we have to be able to see ourselves as women who need some care. For instance, we want to be able to continue to take care of our children or go to work. I can't tell you how important it is that you take and make time for yourself. You won't be able to heal thoroughly without this.

"I said, 'O that I had the wings of a dove! I would fly away and be at rest---I would flee far away and stay in the desert; I would hurry to my place of shelter, far from the tempest and storm.'"(Psalms 55:6)

NOTES:

CLEAN YOUR PLATE

"One thing I ask of the Lord, this is what I seek: that I may dwell in the house of the Lord all the days of my life, to gaze upon the beauty of the Lord and to seek Him in His temple." (Psalms 27:4)

This verse is the bottom line in being whole: seeking God, focusing on Him alone. In the world of recovery it's critical to allow time to "do the work" and to focus on getting healthy and stronger. Maybe it's time to take a serious, critical look at your schedule. If you can't do this, maybe you could have someone help you weed out all of the unnecessary things on your plate. We are all busy doing things that, if the truth were known, we would like to quit doing, but don't know how. Sometimes we allow ourselves to be over-busy so that we can forget and are distracted for a while. Healing takes time and emotional energy that is sucked out of us by busy schedules. People don't really need to hear the whole story of why you're going to drop choir for a while. To say "I just have some other things that need attention right now" is sufficient. Remember, too, that while you may have to set aside some things, it's probably only for a while, not forever.

"Be still, and know that I am God; I will be exalted among the nations, I will be exalted in the earth." (Psalms 46:10)

NOTES:

SIDE BY SIDE

"A friend loves at all times, and a brother is born for adversity."
(Proverbs 17:17)

It's very important for women to have a support system of some
kind, whether it's one or two really good friends, family, or a
support group. We really cannot walk this road of recovery by
ourselves. Eventually, I learned that, but it was quite a while
before I had more than 2 friends who knew what I was going
through. Maybe some of you have already discovered that not
everyone is what we call a "safe" person. If you find that a person
is "unsafe" for you, try not to be discouraged but look more.
Sometimes, people that you think are the closest to you are the
ones who simply cannot handle all the emotion and pain that
you're in. You may hear yourself being blamed in some way for
what is happening. People who have not gone through betrayal
will not be able to understand your pain and why you can't just
"get over it". Real friends are ones that just love on you, are
patient with you, and stand by you even though they haven't
been in the same place you're in. My friends don't just tell me
what I want to hear either, but speak truth into my life with
gentle words. The Holy Spirit is our "Comforter" but He also
provides real flesh and blood women to walk alongside us on our
journey.

*"Two are better than one, because they have a good return for their
work. If one falls down, his friend can help him up. But pity the man
who falls and has no one to help him up." (Ecclesiastes 4:9-10)*

A NEW VIEW

"How can we sing the songs of the Lord while in a foreign land."
(Psalms 137:4)

When crisis strikes, our desire is usually to get things "back to normal" as quickly as possible. I know that was my goal. The day after my husband disclosed his addiction to me, I got up and proceeded to be "normal" by going to garage sales followed by teaching Sunday School the next day. I soon discovered, however, that getting back to normal was going to be harder than I thought. It took me quite a while to finally admit to myself that there was no going back, only forward. I think this was one of many turning points for me because I realized I had to stop living in the past and try to figure out "today". I was going to have to allow myself to learn new things and to look at problems and solutions in a different way. I had to give myself permission to think differently. That didn't come easily because life just seemed thrown up in the air. I really needed to figure out where things belonged. Resisting thinking "outside the box" will only prolong the confusion and you'll be fighting against yourself. Entering new, foreign territory is scary but God has gone there already and is waiting for you. He knows where you are even if you don't.

"O Lord, You have searched me and You know me. You know when I sit and when I rise; You perceive my thoughts from afar. You discern my going out and my lying down' You are familiar with all my ways."
(Psalms 139:1-3)

NOTES:

NOT A POLICEMAN

"A wife of noble character who can find? She is worth far more than rubies." (Proverbs 31:10, 25-27)

A lot of women become overly involved in their husbands' recovery process. They feel an overwhelming need to know where he's been, who he's been talking to, what he looked at on the computer. They look through his wallet to see if there are any suspicious receipts; they check in his drawers for evidence of acting out. There is a great need to protect ourselves from being hurt again so this is a pretty natural response to being thrust into the very unwelcome world of sexual addiction. A wife wears many hats but one that absolutely does not fit is that of a policeman. I can tell you that it does no good for either the husband's recovery or your emotional well-being. Living in a constant state of suspicion, watching his every move is only going to increase the already high anxiety. He really has to be in charge of his own recovery and responsible for his actions before God. Being a wife at this point is hard enough without adding the role of policeman or accountability partner. It's a burden that we were not meant to carry.

"Houses and wealth are inherited from parents, but a prudent wife is from the Lord." (Proverbs 19:14)

NOTES:

OUT OF THE BOAT

"During the fourth watch of the night Jesus went out to them, walking on the lake. 'Lord, if it's You,' Peter replied, 'tell me to come to You on the water. 'Come, He said.'"(Matthew 14:25, 28-29)

The impossible: That is what getting out of the boat, our comfort zone, feels like. Our minds and hearts cry out, "Wait a minute. This isn't safe! You've never done this before!" We tell ourselves we're going to be hurt again or we're making ourselves too vulnerable. The scriptures don't indicate any hesitation in Peter between the time he asked to come out of the boat, Jesus saying, "Come", and actually stepping out. At that moment he trusted Jesus to keep him safe. Maybe that's what it takes" throwing one leg at a time out of the boat, trusting Jesus for just one step. He has promised He'll be with us always. We falter when we look away from His face into the face of pain and sorrow. Maybe we could take just the first step....

"Immediately Jesus reached out His hand and caught him. 'You of little faith,' He said, 'why did you doubt?'"(Matthew 14:31)

NOTES:

IN A FOREIGN COUNTRY

"My comfort in my suffering is this: Your promise renews my life."
(Psalms119:50)

Our heavenly Father is waiting to offer us the comfort only He can provide. Others can listen and cry with us, but only He can give the deepest healing of our hearts and take us on a journey into intimacy with Himself. In the Old Testament book of Deuteronomy, chapter 4, Moses is giving instruction to the Hebrew people about going into the land promised to them by God. He tells them in verse 25 that if, after having lived in the land for a long time, they become corrupt and turn away from God and toward idols, the punishment from God would be to be scattered among people of other nations, separated from God and each other. Then he says in verse 29, "But if from there you seek the Lord your God, you will find Him if you look for Him with all your heart and with all your soul." We have entered the foreign country of recovery, not knowing the language or customs, not having any sense of security, surrounded by the strangers of fear and pain. But God's word tells us that while we are there, we will find God when we seek Him with our whole hearts and souls. That's our part; God does the rest!

"Then maidens will dance and be glad, young men and old as well. I will turn their mourning into gladness; I will give them comfort and joy instead of sorrow." (Jeremiah 31:13)

NOTES: